Homespun Comes Unraveled

...and other adventures from the radical homemaking frontier

by SHANNON HAYES Ph.D.

ALSO AVAILABLE FROM SHANNON HAYES
Cooking Grassfed Beef
Long Way on a Little: An Earth Lover's Companion for Enjoying Meat, Pinching Pennies and Living Deliciously
Radical Homemakers: Reclaiming Domesticity from a Consumer Culture
The Farmer and the Grill
The Grassfed Gourmet

FORTHCOMING FROM SHANNON HAYES
From Here
Angels and Stones

Available at www.ShannonHayes.org,
as well as through most conventional booksellers.

© 2014 by Shannon Hayes
E-Book   ISBN 978-0-9794391-8-6
Print on demand   ISBN 978-0-9794391-9-3

Library of Congress Control Number: 2014912883

Cover and interior design and production: Jill Shaffer
Cover and interior illustrations: © 2014 Jill Webber
E-book Design: David Wogahn, Sellbox
Editor: Bob Hooper
Proof Reader: Steve Hoare, Black Dome Press

Left to Write Press
270 Rossman Valley Rd
Richmondville, NY 12149
www.ShannonHayes.org
518.827.7595

ABOUT LEFT TO WRITE PRESS
Left to Write Press is an initiative of Shannon Hayes and Bob Hooper, who wanted to publish books completely on their own terms, so they could earn a decent return on Shannon's writing without selling their souls. We are now on our sixth book, and we've managed to stick to our guns. Left to Write Press expresses our agenda for an ecologically sound, socially just world, where everyone is well-fed and happy. Now stop reading this small print, and start enjoying our book!

For Saoirse and Ula,
my muses.

Contents

PART IV: Neighbors

PART V: The Culture Clash

PART VI: The Good Life

Acknowledgments

Writing books can be a lonely process, requiring hours upon hours of solitude; but writing a collection of essays is a vastly different matter. Each of these pieces is a result of my immersion in my community, correspondence with my readers, or hours spent laughing or debating with family and friends. To all of the people who touched my life as I wrote each week, I give my thanks.

In addition, special thanks are due to a few others:

❂ To Saoirse and Ula, who honor Mom's compulsion to write, and daily fuel my creative fire with challenging questions and spirited antics.

❂ To my mom and dad, Jim and Adele Hayes, who understand my need to balance farming with writing, and who make sure they don't call me before 8am, so that I have time to do this creative work. Also, thanks to them for calling me (never before 8:01am) each time a blog post goes live with an overlooked spelling error!

❃ To Steve Hoare, Jill Shaffer and Jill Webber, my production team. Over the years we've created a unique style for my books together. I've so appreciated your attention to detail, your commitment to quality, and your talented touches. Thank you for sticking with me. I could never have made it as an independent author without you to help.

❃ To Bob, who comes down every morning and quietly makes coffee while I read these essays aloud, the first audience for every piece I write. You diplomatically soften my language, strengthen my arguments, and push me to keep a daily discipline. You have believed in me from the very beginning, you edit every book, and you still act like you enjoy my writing. Thank you for being my husband, the father of my children, the farm hand, the dish washer, the laundry master, my editor, my love.

And finally, to my blog followers, who come to see me at the website each week, who take the time to let me know that these words matter to them. There are many days when your words of encouragement are more nourishing than food. Thanks for being a steady presence in my life.

Introduction

When Bob and I engaged in a passionate romp on the living room couch one crisp November morning in 2002, we were pretty sure we had agreed to become parents. What we didn't know was that we had just agreed to a career on the front lines of the radical homemaking movement.

For over a year, we had been farming with my parents at Sap Bush Hollow. Seeing ourselves as "gainfully unemployed" (my husband had recently lost his job, and I was fresh out of grad school), we had managed to patch together a bit of farm income with a few different independent enterprises to make enough money to live. We were in the process of figuring out a magical secret that makes itself known to most folks who choose a subsistence life on the land: *if you can produce more than you can consume, then you can get by without needing a lot of conventional income.*

So now we'd gone and gotten ourselves pregnant. We assumed that we would continue in our lifestyle, but that in a few years' time, the school bus would rumble up the road and take our little bundle of joy away each day, leaving us to our agrarian existence.

A lot changes in a woman's body and in her mind during that nine-month gestation period. As my girth expanded, my mind began to see the world differently. A farm girl my whole life, I began to question the conventional path for my new family during prenatal visits to the hospital. I was turned off by all the birthing protocols that seemed, from my experience with the ewes lambing out on our pastures, to have nothing to do with what birthing should be about. At month seven, I walked away from conventional medicine. Within the next eight weeks' time, as my baby rapidly grew, so did my ideas about bringing children into this world. By the time I gave birth to baby Saoirse, I had become *one of "those moms."* You've seen them before—maybe in a local health food store, or at the library—a home birther, an organic food fanatic, an amateur herbalist. I was to become a home schooler. I was seeking to build a new and different world for my child.

But I didn't have a husband drawing down a six-figure income who could support my new maternal passions. We worked on a family farm. At that time, our income was about 200 percent of the poverty level, and it was destined to go down from there if neither of us intended to take on conventional jobs.

We made it work. We expanded the farm business bit by bit. We came up with some pretty good micro-ventures, and our baby daughter was always surrounded by two generations of family. A few years later, we had a second child, Ula.

By this time, I was frequently invited to speak publicly about our way of life on a grassfed livestock farm. And as I did, I began to discern a common assumption that organic food and grassfed meats were meant for a wealthy elite class, not for ordinary folks who cared about food, farming, family, forests, fields and frugality. But my family was a long way from being wealthy, let alone elite. And so were our farm customers. Indeed, I noticed that many of the folks who were buying our grassfed meats were living like us. They were on the cultural fringe, using their money as a tool to vote for the kind of planet and society they wanted to be a part of. They were making a choice to pay my family a living wage for food that we grew conscientiously in harmony with the earth, even though it was almost double the cost of factory farmed food.

If they weren't wealthy, how were they doing it? I soon learned that they, too, like Bob and me, had become producers, rather than mere consumers. All were accomplished home cooks, and applied various other skills: they made their own medicines from their own herbs, they knitted and sewed their clothing and gifts, they kept gardens, fixed their own cars, repaired their toasters, built their own furniture, canned their own vegetables and jams, or kept their own flock of chickens for their morning eggs.

But the cultural identity of our country portrayed to the rest of the world suggested that people like this didn't exist in our nation. According to magazines and TV ads, Americans are happiest with their iDevices, their fancy cars, credit cards, shopping malls, their Starbucks and McDonalds, pharmaceutical drugs and throw-away dinner plates.

In spite of this conventional image, I began looking for a different America . . . the one I was seeing in my own farm customer base. In 2008, I began researching this alternative culture. Through extensive interviews and travel, I discovered more members of the same tribe. Their lives, intentionally and profoundly centered around the family's well-being, were informed by a keen awareness of global politics. They were focusing on home, hearth, and domestic skills as a way to restore balance to their world. Rather than simply "stay-at-home" moms and dads, these folks were living deliberate lives with deep philosophical underpinnings for their daily choices. For that reason, I came up with the moniker *Radical Homemakers*.

When my book by that title was released, our little family was thrown into the limelight. We were asked to appear on national television, we became the subjects of photo essays, our story was told in major national and international newspapers and magazines. What started out as a quiet life guided by our ideals and intentions was suddenly a subject of national fascination. We were regarded as some kind of bizarre anomaly to mainstream American Culture.

But Bob and I knew that we weren't bizarre (at least not in this regard!). We were part of something that was much larger than ourselves. We were building on a long national tradition of using self-reliance as a means for bringing about political change. This first happened with the American Revolutionary War. The cultivation of household self-reliance enabled Americans to boycott products bearing taxes they felt were unfair. When the British military cut off Boston harbor, the self-reliance of neighboring villages and states kept the city from starving. We can talk about the Revolutionary War itself as a means for political change, but our colonies never could have declared themselves a nation were it not for the domestic self-reliance of its citizens.

Under the tutelage of Helen and Scott Nearing, these ideals re-emerged again in the 1960s and 1970s with the back-to-the-land movement. Young Americans grew outraged about our nation's industrialized food system, our domineering global politics, our warfare, our rapidly expanding culture of consumerism. The Nearings, in their pursuit of a form of self-reliance that enabled them to live in peace with the earth and all her inhabitants, inspired countless Americans to pursue a hearth-centered existence on the land. The governing principle was that, by living a life of non-exploitation committed to social justice, a person could become a force for change in this world.

Today's radical homemakers carry that torch forward. However, economics have changed a lot from the 1960s and 1970s. Not everyone who dreams of cultivating a life of self-reliance as a way to free the world from climate emissions, polluted soil and water and social injustices can afford to buy a patch of land in the country. Not everyone wants to. Today's radical homemakers, I found, were living in cities, where they operated guerrilla gardens on city property and on their rooftops; in suburbs, where they flouted local zoning ordinances

4

against hanging their laundry outdoors to dry; as well as in the country, where, like Bob, me, and my parents, they have devoted themselves to creating a socially and ecologically sound food system.

But that story didn't come across in the media blitz that followed the release of *Radical Homemakers*. Radical Homemakers, to the media, were just a new brand of quirky modern hippie. But the letters that came pouring in to our home from kindred spirits across the country told me that that there were a lot of us. And in order to make ourselves into a movement, we needed a forum for conversation.

At the request of *Yes! Magazine*, the publication of a non-profit organization dedicated to positive social change, I agreed to begin a series of monthly online essays about our radical homemaking lifestyle. At their encouragement, I didn't need to write a series of "how to be self-reliant" stories, nor did I need to amass a collection of political polemics about the "whys" of what we do. Rather, the editors felt that, in order for the movement to grow, in order for fellow radical homemakers to find each other, and in order for more people to begin pursuing lives of non-exploitation, social justice and sustainability, I simply needed to start talking in an illustrative way, about my life. They invited me to simply be a story teller, to let folks know about the ordinary happenings in my world, and to explore how, as a radical homemaker, I worked my way through them.

And so the stories began to come forward. It was slow going, at first. But soon, as I connected more with readers and their questions, I began writing with more frequency, and publishing them on my own blog at ShannonHayes.org, as well as through *Yes!*

I learned to share stories about the little things, the daily details in my radical homemaking life that captured the how, the why, and the heart of what Bob and I do. I soon learned that allowing our vulnerabilities, mistakes, hypocrisies and imperfections to play a part in the story telling helped to make them more accessible. Sometimes they are quite comedic. Sometimes I do offer some practical tips. Other times,

I recount stories of sadness. In doing this, I wanted to paint a picture of a way of life, but I didn't want to sell it only for its glossy, lovely side. I wanted anyone who considered it to be aware of the grit, confusion, and struggle that also plays a part in all this raw beauty. This is a good way of life. It is a path that has kept me and my family very happy and economically secure, even in times of great crisis. But like every life, it is not perfect, and these stories invite you to see that.

It has been over ten years since that romp on the living room couch that led us to have Saoirse, that led us to become radical homemakers, that led us, unwittingly, to the forefront of a movement. And while I never foresaw such an unfolding as I was wrapped in my husband's arms, I am just as passionate about the outcome as I was during that bright November morning.

Home Economics

Harvest Hoarder Syndrome

The last of the tomato plants will go into the ground at our farm this week. Meanwhile, the first ripe tomatoes of the season showed up at our farmers' market on Saturday (how do they DO that?). Thus, it was with a fair degree of confidence that I descended the stairs into my basement last night to retrieve one of my precious jars of homemade canned tomato sauce.

When I got down there, 30 jars of tomato sauce sat on the shelves before me. At the rate my family uses tomato sauce, that equates to a 12- to 18-month supply still sitting in my basement at the start of a new tomato season. There is also a 3-year supply of dilly beans, 2-year supply of canned peaches, and 2-year supply of pickled beets. I still have a case of lamb stew I canned three years ago, 15 jars of plums I canned in 2006 or 2007, and several jars of pickles of various flavors. My freezer is in similar condition. I put away 16 quarts of fresh raspberries last summer (13 remain, and the fruit has already set on my bushes for this year), 10 quarts of blueberries, which were added to the 15 quarts of blueberries I'd put away from the summer before, 5 quarts of strawberries (when they are fresh and abundant right now), 1½ gallons of rhubarb I've held for 4 years (again, presently growing rampantly in my garden), and several quarts of frozen corn, dehydrated tomatoes, beans and peppers. In my refrigerator, I also still have 1½ gallons of fermented cortido, kimchee, and sauerkraut.

The time has come for me to admit the embarrassing truth: My name is Shannon, and I'm a Harvest Hoarder. The burgeoning of the new growing season has begun, and I still have enough food stored for a few more years. The condition results from three primary causes:

1. I worked so damned hard putting that food up that I'm overly parsimonious about using it.

2. I keep forgetting that the food is down there and fail to bring it up to share with my family and friends . . . and continually buy new, fresh (albeit usually local) ingredients instead, wasting the precious dollars I claimed to save through my food preservation efforts.

3. I harbor apocalyptic fantasies in my brain wherein I am able to feed my family for a prolonged period of time with no ability to acquire fresh food. Everyone will live through a traumatic period of blizzards, electromagnetic surges, locusts, or a zombie attack, owing to my back stock of pickled beets.

Of course, there is some wisdom to this practice. We don't grocery shop often, and having stored food carries us over when 6-8 weeks slip by between trips to our co-op, an hour's drive from home. An alien spaceship could wipe out transit routes and we could still eat for a little while longer. Or, something more believable could happen—such as a hurricane and flood that causes our valley farms to go 8 feet under water in the height of the growing season, which happened a few years back.

Losing the entirety of our local food supply in one afternoon makes a lasting impression. And having a full larder of preserved foods when all roads and electricity were shut down during that traumatic week was comforting for my family. My kids still remember hurricane Irene as "that day we had melting ice cream for breakfast!"

But I've gone too far. Keeping a back stock on hand even in the height of abundance is wise. But holding onto several years' supply in the basement while buying fresh fruits and vegetables is an absurd waste of money, labor, jars, lids, freezer bags, fuel and food. Hoarding beyond reasonable need is its own form of wasteful consumerism.

I am still coming up the learning curve on my personal path to self-reliance, and I am growing keenly aware of the fine balance between preparedness and resilience, and the importance of not littering one's life with fears of an unknown future. At this point, I'd argue that excess stored food beyond one year's supply is probably tipping the balance toward a paranoid clutter. There comes a point where I need to put some trust in the cycles of nature and my future: that I will find time to can again, that someone will share my values enough to help me with the labor, that the harvest will return.

I suppose this amounts to surrendering myself to a certain degree of trust, faith and hope, which could be extended into many areas of my life beyond my kitchen canner. How much more sustainable would this planet be if we could trust that there will be enough food, enough money, enough love, enough help to have our needs met in this life? We could be living with a lot less fear. And living with less fear would enable us to live with more generosity. And living with more generosity would enable all of us to benefit from the surplus frozen corn and canned green beans. And that ability to share and trust would make the preserved harvest taste all the more sweet.

Pickled beets, anyone?

Radical Investing

I received a phone call recently from someone in the media, who introduced himself, then exclaimed, "Is what I read true . . . that you have a family of four and live on less than $45,000 per year? And if so, how is that POSSIBLE?"

Actually, it wasn't true. This year, we lived on less than $30,000. My husband Bob doesn't call me the "Cheap Mick" for nothing.

Soon after, I received an email from a reader who had just come into an inheritance from her mother. She wanted my advice on how to invest it responsibly.

My first reaction, of course, was that I'm the wrong person to ask. I'm definitely not an expert on how to spend money. I'm more of an expert in how *not* to spend money.

I glanced over at my financial calculations scratched on the back-side of a post-it note (yes, even they get re-used). It's definitely been a tough year for cash flow, but it certainly hasn't felt like our family has been living on so little money. We have a lovely home, we eat well, we have lots of fun, we're warm, and we don't worry about how we'll keep the lights on.

For me, that should be the objective when investing money. Our culture typically instructs us to think of investing in terms of generating interest, so that we'll have more money, so that we can invest more money, and eventually have a higher income as a result. It assumes a continual growth of the economy. Bob and I believe that to expect that our economy can (or should) be in a state of continual growth is an impossible and unsustainable notion.

Our family financial goals are different. When we have enough money to invest, we want to use it in a way that, rather than make more money, will directly enable us to enjoy a good quality of life in perpetuity—no matter what happens in the mainstream economy; no matter what weather extremes we may face; and no matter what our annual income happens to be in any given year. Knowing this about our financial philosophy, here is how I would advise anyone to think about investing the occasional cash windfall:

Lower your cost of living. First and foremost, this means paying off any interest-bearing debts. Monthly payments of any kind rack up the monthly income demands, and you get nothing in exchange for paying interest. Paying off interest-bearing debt is a guaranteed return on your investment—you'll probably never find any investment that will pay you, say, 12 percent interest, so instead, try to lose the thing that *costs* you that amount. Get rid of credit card payments, pay off the student loans and car loan, get rid of the mortgage, or pay it all down as much as possible. Once you've eliminated all debt, turn your attention to lowering your household expenses. When Bob and I have had the extra cash, we've used it for a better replacement wood stove, solar hot water and electricity, blown-in insulation, and replacement windows. We've also used it to do upkeep on our house, so that we're not panicking about a leaking roof at a time when cash flow may be in the negative. For some folks, this might even mean buying a home in a place where the cost of living is cheaper, or moving closer to a job to cut down transportation costs.

Invest in your ability to produce. One of my core mantras is "Produce, don't consume." By producing for our basic needs and pleasures, we lower our cost of living, reduce our ecological impact and occupy ourselves with activities that are a lot more enjoyable and satisfying than simply buying things in the marketplace. And when you are busy making what you need and/or love, you don't have much time to think about spending money. Producing can also generate income. Bob and I produce our own honey, candles, soaps, and ointments to cut our household expenses, but the surplus sales of these items pay our property taxes. Investing in production may be something small, like garden seeds, a stockpot to make broth, or blueberry bushes, laying hens or asparagus crowns, all of which will lower food bills. It might mean investing money to start a micro-enterprise (a few years back we invested a few thousand dollars and began a value-added wool business with our sheep's fleeces), or buying tools you need to build, fix or mend things.

In our family, one of our most important financial investments was in an expansive working kitchen that includes two cooktops (one, high-efficiency electric and one gas that can work in power outages), several large sinks and several yards of counter space. We created a space where a stockpot can be simmering, a meal can be prepared and a bushel of beets can be pickled, all at the same time that clean-up is going on (if you've ever bristled at the irony of having to order take-out on the nights you are canning, you can appreciate such an investment). That same kitchen lets us do our production crafts while running recipe tests, and still allows for the kids to run through and make themselves a snack or grab a glass of water.

An investment in production might be something pleasurable, as well. In fact, during the winter months, when our cash flow nearly stops, it is probably one of our most important investments. Bob owns a couple of musical instruments, which he loves to play. He spends hours in the winter strumming his guitar or plucking his mandolin, making lovely music (we consider these "sound investments"). I have my recorders, and we all sing. I once spent a over one hundred dollars on a set of high-quality interchangeable knitting needles, with which I've knitted several miles of our farm's wool (and saved a lot of money on some great Christmas gifts). When we sit by the fire and he plays music and I knit, neither one of us craves a fancy dinner out, more fashionable clothing, vacations, or the newest iPhone. Heck, with the exception of Saturday nights (when we do like to indulge in a single martini), we don't even feel the urge to drink. Cheap fun is priceless.

Invest in your security. Even though they seem like lousy investments, I'm a big fan of certificates of deposit (CDs) through local banks and credit unions. I'm the extreme epitome of a "conservative investor." More than once I've had it explained to me how I can have far superior rates of return by using more sophisticated investment instruments. My answer is always the same: My ability to save can outpace any rate of return you can find in the financial markets. Therefore, I'd prefer to see my savings as secure as possible. Certificates of deposit are insured, they allow for emergency cash if the wolf is truly at the door, yet they are conveniently locked away and inaccessible enough to make it difficult to simply withdraw them on a whim.

If, like me, you are living in a place that seems to be falling victim to extreme climate events, investing in your security might also mean putting some funds toward increasing your self-reliance, with things like generators, hand pumps, gas cooktops, wood stoves, and the like. It's good to stay warm, dry, fed and hydrated when all the roads in your county are shut down and the power's gone.

Invest in the economy that surrounds you. My parents have long taught me the value of this practice, and as they've come into the years when they have extra capital, they have consistently directed it into the local community. They've used their extra capital to provide friends and neighbors with mortgages, underwrite entrepreneurial ventures, finance home improvements, or just help someone to buy a car to get to work. They do collect interest on their loans, but always far less than a bank charges. Our local food co-op recently ran a campaign to encourage the members to finance an expansion, and our entire family invested in that, as well. Local investment opportunities can be more lucrative than CDs or formal socially responsible investment forums (our personal "local" loans have generated anywhere from 1-6 percent interest, as opposed to the current 0.40 percent of a 3-year bank CD, or 1-3 percent for a socially responsible investment firm), but they are only as safe as your judge of character. They are also contingent upon being deeply embedded within a community, where the social networks help to guarantee payments (there are times when my folks have had to make a few pestering phone calls in order to keep payments on schedule), but they are empowered to show more forgiveness and flexibility than a national bank chain bureaucracy. In an effort to facilitate more local connections, an organization called Slow Money has developed a movement of community chapters that set up local entrepreneurial showcases where private investors can meet with sustainable food entrepreneurs. Their website contains links to these chapters, as well as links to other like-minded social investment opportunities. You can learn more at www.slowmoney.com.

So there are my thoughts and suggestions when it comes to investing money responsibly. The returns are pretty small. When I do have money to invest, I try to strike an average return of 3 percent, and even that might be higher than what I can expect in the future. But when you can make money work for you more than you work for it, you begin to gauge returns in a broader sense than mere dollars. If I can keep my family's costs of living down, and we can continue to produce things we need to survive and enjoy life, I think we'll be okay. Of course, that doesn't mean I don't keep researching and trying to learn more. In fact, I have recorded copious notes on the back side of these used post-its that collect beside my computer.

The Coffee Robot

I was speaking at a conference two weeks ago when a woman approached me requesting that I sign her tattered copy of *Radical Homemakers*. I was pleased to see it so well-used. While I was thinking about what to write, she began to chronicle some of her own radical homemaking dilemmas.

"I really agree with what you say. I really don't want to be a consumer anymore. But sometimes, it's just so . . . so hard. Sometimes there's just something I really want to buy."

I nodded, understanding. "Like our coffee robot."

"Your what?"

The coffee robot is an embarrassing piece of gourmet technology hogging up exactly three square feet of my kitchen counter. I like to blame Bob for its acquisition back in 2005, since he was the one who first fell in love with it. But I was certainly a willing accomplice in the crime. It made an absolutely transformative, perfect cup of coffee. Instantly. All that long summer before we bought it, we talked about it, dreamt about it, and rationalized about it. We'd walk into the gourmet kitchen store to gaze at it as we saved up the exorbitant funds the machine would require. On Saturday mornings, when we rose at

5 a.m. to get ready for our farmers' market, we fantasized about how deliciously pleasant it would be to start our day with that perfect cup of coffee (or espresso . . . *or* cappuccino). We scraped together our pennies, and by Christmas we had it.

We were frugal radical homemakers even then. And we used that logic to justify the purchase. Having such a machine would keep us from buying coffee out (never mind that the nearest place to buy a decent cup of coffee is one hour's drive away . . . and hence we *never* went out for coffee anyhow). We could help another friend conserve resources by giving her our old drip pot, and we'd save trees by not buying filters, and our happiness would immeasurably improve.

Well, our friends' lives *did* improve. They loved coming over for a cup of coffee. But since the stupid machine could only brew one cup at a time (or two cups at half the speed), they sat and chatted, while poor Bob played barista and ran back and forth between the kitchen table and the coffee robot. By the time he'd filled every guest's mug and then drawn his own cup, at least half the people at the table would be ready for a refill. And, of course, the machine was too technical to allow a guest to simply get up and make their own . . .

Admittedly, the coffee was delicious. And convenient, if there was only one person drinking. Bob was able to have as much perfect coffee as he wanted while he worked around the house. All day long I would hear that machine winding up, grinding a fresh cup, and spewing forth Bob's favorite caffeinated elixir. Beginning to grow suspicious of the sound, I secretly counted the number of cups of coffee Bob drank one day, and when I observed he'd consumed a half gallon of the stuff, I abandoned my covert research and screamed at him that he was forcing himself into adrenal failure. As if to underscore my point, he *very quickly* screamed back a stream of vituperation.

And the money savings? It's true that we never went out for coffee, just like before. And we certainly saved that $28 per year on paper filters. But we spent over $100 per year instead on plastic specialty filters and water purifying tablets, which required an hour-long drive to Albany to purchase. Plus, we doubled our expenditure on coffee (albeit organic and fair-trade, of course).

Then, the coffee robot broke. Bob immediately called the company and began arranging for service and repairs, which would start at $250, "depending on what's wrong with it." Meanwhile, I fished our old French press pot out of our camping gear and heated water on the stove. We brought the pot out into the sun, sat down together and . . . Wow! That stuff—four cups at once—was really good!

The coffee robot still sits on our counter, broken, an embarrassing relic of consumerism.

And I think it may very well have been one of the best purchases Bob and I ever made. Not, of course, because of its dependability, nor because of the quality of the coffee, but because it forced us to reflect about how we spend our money.

When we buy consumer goods, very often we are trying to buy dreams, packaged in plastic and electronics. Bob and I didn't need a coffee robot. We wanted time together experiencing something pleasurable. We wanted to spend more time enjoying the company of our friends. We wanted to spend more time relaxing. We bought a coffee robot, when what we really wanted was time to sit and drink coffee. What we ended up losing in exchange was money *and* time.

That's been an important lesson for us. Consumer compulsions don't fade easily, especially when catalogs and advertising show up daily in the mailbox, the inbox, and the cyber pop-up box. And even though Bob and I espouse honorable values about preserving the earth's resources, we know first-hand how easy it is to get swallowed up by the lure of new, life-enhancing products.

But there sits the coffee robot. And when we ponder getting an iPhone, or a piece of furniture, or (heaven forbid) a new kitchen gadget, that clunky monument to our folly reminds us to think more carefully about what it is we're truly pining for when we feel compelled to make a purchase.

In the long run, I guess the coffee robot really did save us money. Having made such a stupid mistake already, we find ourselves repeating it much less often. When tempted by consumer goods, we find ourselves often saying "hmmm . . . but will that really make us happier?" And we understand now what "making us happier" really means. For us, "happier" means our lives are made less complicated, that we are able to spend more time together as a family, more time doing creative work, and less time running errands or worrying about money.

Thus, now that we understand that lesson, I guess I can honestly say that the coffee robot did, in a roundabout way, make us happier. Of course, it would make me happier still if I could get rid of the damned thing and get back some of my counter space.

Of Songs and Suppers

"Can we invite Cyndi Lauper over for dinner?" Ula asks.

Occasionally, my children's dim understanding of reality surprises me. I am standing in the kitchen, searing pieces of beef before flicking them in the slow cooker to make a stew for Saturday at the market. She will be accompanying me, even though the forecast is for rain.

Usually, she and her sister are happy to spend market days home on the farm with their grandparents, helping with chores, baking when the weather is foul, or swimming or fishing when the days are warm. But I have a suspicion that they have decided market sales require closer supervision this year. They are now in business for themselves. They have a babysitting business, a dog biscuit enterprise, and Ula is marketing her own line of greeting cards. They are pooling all their funds in a vacation jar, which is already bursting with $1300 from their efforts over the last eight months.

It is supposed to be my job to manage their sales at the farmers' market. But when I came home the first week and had no greeting card or dog biscuit figures to report, I think they may have held a private shareholders' meeting to discuss the problem. Ula, the ace sales-woman, has since decided to accompany me to help boost business. When babysitting gigs come up, Saoirse will hold down the fort, caring for their charge at the farm.

I already feel as though I am on some sort of probation when Ula asks to invite Cyndi over for dinner. I don't like repeatedly being a disappointment to my children.

"No," I tell her flatly. "I'm not inviting Cyndi Lauper over for dinner."

"Because the house is so messy?"

"Actually, we don't know her."

Occasionally, her mother's dim understanding of reality surprises Ula. I see her shake her head to herself. She has no response for me.

The next day at the market, business begins to pick up. Ula perches on a stool behind the booth, greeting people with a wide smile.

"Can I help you?" she asks.

"I was looking for some chopped meat," one customer takes this seven-year-old up on her solicitous offer.

"Well that's over here." She points to the spot in the booth where we display the ground beef. "But we also sell dog biscuits, and I made them myself."

And she gets a sale.

Before noon, she's sold two packs of greeting cards and her entire stock of dog biscuits. In light of her hard work (and in the interest of getting her out of my hair for a while), I let her take a little of her earnings and put it in her pocket. She charges out of the booth, ready to feed the local economy. I am busy selling pork roasts and chickens, so I don't pay much attention.

The crowd is thick just after twelve o'clock. The rain must have led people to sleep in, and they are coming in to the market later than usual. I barely notice the guitar player who has begun strumming down in the pavilion. One of my customers gestures down to the scene.

"Is that your daughter down there dancing?"

I don't even look up. "Probably," I say, keeping my attention focused on tallying sales. I'm grateful for the live music. It is the perfect distraction for my Ula. Otherwise, now that she's sold out of product, she'll keep pestering me to buy sweets.

A little while later, there is a break in the crush, and I am re-stocking the table. Ula comes running up to me.

"Mommy! Mommy! Did you hear the music down there? It's great! I took all my money and I gave it to the other kids who were listening, so they could give it to the guitar player!"

Now she had my attention. "You did *what?*"

"I gave it to the other kids."

"You just gave it to kids you didn't know?"

"Yeah. I gave it to them so they could pay the guitar player." Another customer comes up to buy eggs.

"Ula! You can't DO that!" My voice is a sharp hiss, my eyes fierce with that *Mom Glare*—The one that is intended to restore order at times when I have to behave myself in front of the outside world and *seem* nice *and* in control of my children.

Her eyes grow wide when she sees my disappointment in her. She stammers a bit. "I– I– I thought the kids should pay for the music." I see little tears in the corners of her eyes. "I'm sorry Mommy!"

I feel a sudden lead weight in my stomach. *I am not handling this correctly.* I'm not sure what to say. As is often the case, Ula has once more caught me off guard with unforeseen challenges to my parenting policy. I know I have done something wrong, but another customer is approaching, and I have no time to think things through. At a total loss, I throw my arms around her and kiss her cheek, then whisper "You are loving and generous. You are not a bad person. We'll talk about this later."

I am thinking all the following week that I need to teach Ula more skills about controlling her impulses, about planning her spending, about understanding how hard she has worked for her dollars, and the importance of saving them. But I don't find time to discuss it.

The next weekend, an accordion, fiddler and saxophonist come to the market. Saoirse joins her sister on the sales force. After they've moved sufficient product, I see both of them out on the lawn, twirling and twisting to the music. Knowing that I had a problem with her handing dollars over to perfect strangers, Ula tosses half her money into the accordian case. She hands the other half to Saoirse, who happily throws it in. This time, I say nothing.

This past week, my friend Lisa, a fellow homeschooling mom, comes for lunch. Our girls run and play outside, and our mommy conversation turns to celebrity worship; about our culture's tendency to appoint rock stars, movie stars, pre-teen and teen idols to incite infatuation among American youth . . . to get them to pine for the fame and fortune that will be allotted to so few.

"Saoirse and Ula have never really known about that," I observe. "There are lots of local musicians around, and they just *know* them." I gave it some more thought. "I mean, they love what they do, they love going out to hear them play. But they don't think of them as demigods, or anything."

Lisa leans forward. "You mean, they see them as ordinary, hard-working people, like everyone else."

Her comment stays with me throughout the day after she has left. *They see them as ordinary, hard working people, like everyone else.* My mind keeps flitting back to the scene on Ula's first day at the farmers' market. Ula had worked hard. She had made greeting cards. She had made dog biscuits. She had mustered her courage and talked to potential customers about her product. She had made sales. And down in the pavilion, there was a musician, bringing music to the market, filling our community space with joyful, dancing children.

That musician worked hard. For every three-minute song he played, he had to invest a lifetime in lessons and practice.

In farm business accounting, we learn about calculating return to labor. Farmers raise products, keep track of their costs, determine the price (if they are direct marketers), and any profit is considered a "return to labor," the actual payment we see for the time invested. Depending on the enterprise, we see anywhere from $2 to $10 per hour. And as a vociferous advocate for the rights of farmers to earn a fair wage, I never hesitate to share those shockingly low figures.

But what is the return to labor for ordinary, non-celebrity musicians? On that day at the market, did they make anything more for their efforts than the money my seven-year-old was sending into their cases?

My friend Lisa was right. Ula saw the musicians as hard-working people. *Just like herself.* And she sent her cash, that representation of her own life energy, into their instrument cases. Ula valued the music as much as she valued her own labor. It was as important to her as any other locally-made product on offer at that market.

Local music and arts—the documenting of the culture, history, and struggles in our own backyards—have tremendous value to my children. It celebrates *their* place in this world. It does not drive them to pine for elite stardom. Instead, it brings them closer to home. And rather than seeing musicians as separate from themselves, Saoirse and Ula regard them as part of our community and our local economy, as a source for their energy to dance through life.

Thus, I suppose it is only natural for Ula to want to invite Cyndi Lauper over for dinner. It is true that we've never met her, and that we only have her albums, but since other musicians work hard and perform at the farmers' market, at the library, in our local church hall, or out in the parks, Cyndi must do the same, right? And if Cyndi works hard to put out good music, shouldn't she be rewarded with a good home-cooked meal, straight from the farm? It only seems fair.

This week, in preparation for the market, I sit down with Ula and the money jar. I point to the wadded up bills pressing against the glass.

"Ok, Ula. This money stays in the jar. It is your savings. But this," I pull out a stack of ones and count them into her hand, "is for the market."

I have learned that I am not always the best arbiter of her pecuniary decisions. "Spend it on whatever you like. When it's gone, it is gone. But it *is* your choice. If you want to give it to kids to pay the musicians, that's fine."

"But you said I shouldn't do that."

"I was wrong. You were doing something important, and I didn't understand."

She smiles and jumps up and down with pleasure, relieved that my dim understanding of reality has brightened somewhat. I suppose it is only a matter of time before she broaches the subject of fixing supper for Cyndi once more. Because now, hopefully, I'll understand her view on the matter—*Every musician needs to eat.*

Family

Company Coming

$\mathcal{I}$ wouldn't say I'm a slob, exactly. The toilets get scrubbed, I'm a champion when it comes to de-cluttering (once the debris piles reach a critical mass), and the sheets get changed regularly. But I do possess a certain, ummm . . . *grime blindness*. Since most cobwebs are above my sightline, I don't notice them. The windows were last washed in 2008. Dusting really only occurs on those surfaces that see the most activity. I consider a healthy dirt population vital stimulation for my family's immune system.

It's not quite the same for Bob. Maybe it's because he is significantly taller, so he sees more of the dust and cobwebs from up there. Maybe (most likely) it has something to do with his WASPy New England roots.

And while the vacuum cleaner is one of his personal power tools—and he wields it with truly sexy masculine form—he generously lets the rest slide with only occasional gurgles of frustration . . . until a visit with company is on the horizon.

A few months ago, we learned that our good friends, the Bowies, would be visiting from England for one week this August. Bob began planning right away. Our house, the color of grayed-over untreated pine siding, was slowly stained an earthy brown with burgundy trim over the course of the summer. Our front porch was cleared of tools and lumber scraps. Deteriorating screen doors were repaired. In an effort to match his enthusiasm, I bought flowers for the front deck and attempted to keep them fertilized and watered. I stacked the firewood early.

As the days before their arrival grew fewer, Bob's efforts grew more intense. During each spare moment, he would work at re-shelving books, cleaning up his basket weaving supplies, re-organizing the guest room. And then, he'd step out to where the girls and I were doing our best to stay out of his way . . . and moan at our mess. Saoirse's yarn and felt scraps littered our floor. The contents of the costume bag were strewn across the living room. Both girls seem to regard tooth brushing as a crafting hobby for re-surfacing the bathroom sink and mirror. Ula is in the phase where she likes to pull all clothes out of drawers and scatter them across the bedroom floor as she puts together new outfits every 20 minutes. Clean and dirty five-year-old's undies and socks get mixed together and wind up in the most unexpected locations—under couch cushions, under desks, outside on the deck.

I'm not much better. No sooner are the leftovers from the last meal stored away than I have to begin cooking the next meal or testing the next recipe. The lamb harvest is coming in and there is fat to render, the bones need straining from the meat broth, and a few jars of fermented pickles sit out on the counter bubbling over and threatening to mold. My desk is a clutter of articles, books, receipts, bills; stained, splattered, and jotted-over recipes; phone messages, and disseminated important scribbles for future masterpieces jotted sideways and on the backs of envelopes and reused paper. The contents spill over to the floor, confusing themselves with junk mail and wastepaper in such a way that no one but me is authorized to touch it.

Tensions were starting to grow last week with only 7 days until the Bowies' arrival. I was working at my desk, the kids were on the carpet behind me, and Bob walked through, looked at our detritus and actually moaned with anxiety.

My temper grew short. "We can't just stop living to keep the house nice!" I snapped at him. He growled a few choice words back.

In spite of my defensiveness, I fully understood how he felt. I wanted our house to look nice, too. It only needed to be "perfect" just for one quiet moment when we brought the Bowies home. As long as we held together long enough to make a good first impression, we would both be satisfied. He wasn't asking for too much.

Saoirse and Ula can be recruited to help out to a certain degree, but their creativity and unwillingness to part with a single paper scrap usually make them an obstruction to progress. Rather than cleaning their craft areas, they turn it into gallery time, figuring out how to tape every little art project to the walls of the house. They set about picking up their toys upstairs, but soon decide that "cleaning" means meticulously arranging them in interesting and artful scenes from their imagination. At the same time, my being on the cusp of releasing a new book as the fall meat harvest begins keeps my farm, computer and desk demands high. Thus, so long as I must work, my office chaos is nearly impossible to contain.

The climax in our house cleaning drama happened Wednesday morning, just three days prior to the Bowies' long-anticipated arrival. Bob and I sat staring at each other over a cup of coffee, trying to arrange how much cleaning could get done that morning before we had to go down to the farm and report for the fresh chicken sale later that afternoon. Saoirse came in, threw a blanket and a pillow down on the floor and laid down in front of us. Ula followed with a few choice toys. They began to squabble. The puppy appeared from behind my rocking chair and coughed up a few shards of my bamboo knitting needles on the rug. The phone started to ring. Bob dropped his head in his hands. I began chewing my lip. I ordered the kids to go back upstairs and took the phone call while I silently prayed for a fairy godmother to come help us resolve our chaotic distress. Apparently she was listening. And had a cruel sense of humor.

Suddenly, Saoirse threw up—strawberry yogurt, I think. She didn't make it to the toilet in time, and it looked like a murder scene upstairs. And there, in the midst of the worst mess imaginable at that point, lay our blessing. Saoirse stopped moving. She lay down in her bed and fell asleep. We tackled her craft table without her protests. A vomiting child is a legitimate excuse to get out of helping at the chicken pick-up, so Bob was able to stay home and continue cleaning while Ula and I went down to the farm to work.

And while we were there, Ula threw up. And while Saoirse likes to retreat to a dark corner and have no one come near her when she is sick, Ula has different requirements. She wants Mommy by her side for the entire length of the illness. Suddenly, I couldn't deal with customers, I couldn't deal with emails, and Ula was too sick for me to move her back home. We retreated upstairs in the farmhouse, far away from the customers, and tended to her woes. Bob's day suddenly got a whole lot better. His loving mess makers, one wife and two children, were suddenly occupied with a stomach bug. Life came to a temporary standstill. No cooking needed to be done, no toys could be taken out, no craft projects were attempted. Laundry was done, beds were made, dust bunnies and cobwebs were removed.

The girls recovered quickly, but their energy levels were low enough that we were able to catch up. The Bowies were scheduled to arrive Saturday morning. Steady progress was made each hour until then. When Saturday dawned, we decided Bob would go to our farmers' market, and I would stay home with the kids to retrieve our guests from the train station. He smiled over his coffee that morning, looking at the vacuumed, (mostly) dusted, de-cluttered, fresh-sheeted, de-cobwebbed, painted house with the pretty not-dead-yet (but well on their way) flowers out front. It was the best we were going to do. Satisfied, he kissed me, then picked up his cash box and vaulted down the steps to the car.

I waved to him as he left, then went about my checklist. There was dinner to get ready for tonight, and then the meat for Sunday's meal needed to be seared and put in the slow cooker. It would only generate a few dishes and some minor grease splatters. Hopefully I'd be able to get them washed before it was time to leave . . . and then Ula came downstairs and reported a bed-wetting accident. And so there was a load of laundry to do, and then that would have to be hung out before we left. And then Saoirse and Ula decided to make a few welcome cards and crafts as gifts for their arrival, which meant a few snips of paper and yarn and felt here and there . . . .and a box of crayons left out on the couch. Nothing too major, right?

I did my best to hold the place together according to Bob's vision while he was gone. I straightened up the screen porch, vacuumed out the loft, finished making up all the guest beds. But the laundry wasn't going to be dry in time to take inside. Undies, t-shirts and bed sheets would be flapping in the breeze to greet the Bowies upon their arrival. The craft table would once again be littered with an assortment of heart-felt scraps. I smiled as we headed out the door to retrieve our British friends. Our home is an ecosystem, and no matter how perfect we'd like to make it, as long as we live and create there, it will never be sterile, still and clean. But our long-time friends would soon be with us, and the joy of their arrival quickly overshadowed all concerns about our messy, happy house.

As they came inside with their luggage, they looked about and sighed, "What a perfectly lovely home! I *do* hope you didn't go to any trouble."

Bullying: Can it teach us anything about ourselves?

*S*aoirse and Ula have a favorite family story they are forever asking me to retell. It is about my first encounter with bullies in my kindergarten year. It goes like this: At the end of each day, my older brother and his best friend would pick me up from my classroom, and together we'd walk to our babysitter's house in town. And each day, the moment we were off school property, three bullies waited for us. For a period of time, they made threats, and we just kept walking. But the afternoon eventually came when fighting ensued. Each of the two older boys took on my brother and his friend. They instructed the youngest to "get the girl."

I stared at him coming at me. Owing to earlier advice given by my mother, I dropped my backpack off my shoulder, which held a metal lunch pail. I kept the strap in my hand. As soon as he was close enough, I closed my eyes and swung in a circle, clobbering the first thing that came into contact with the lunch pail and bag, which was the boy's head. Golly, did he let out a wail. The cry was loud enough to break up the other two fights, and the three bullies went home to tell on me. No trouble ever came of the incident, and we were able to walk safely to the babysitter's house after that.

The story is one of my most vivid childhood memories, as it was the end of my fear of bullies. Oh, how innocent it all was back then.

Flash forward to my early twenties, when I was working as a high school English teacher in Japan, with 600 students. As an adult, I never saw the bullying. But one of my students wound up committing suicide over it. Naturally, by the time I had children of my own, the idea of childhood bullying struck me as horrific. And while bully avoidance wasn't the reason I chose to homeschool my kids, I was perfectly happy to sidestep that part of Saoirse's and Ula's growing pains.

It turns out I didn't sidestep it as much as I thought.

Saoirse was recently invited to an overnight sleepover party at her best friend's house, where she and three other girls spent the night outside in a tent. I picked up a smiling, rosy-cheeked girl the next morning, full of laughter and spirit. A few days later, when we had an opportunity to have lunch alone together, I asked her to tell me all about it.

"It was really fun, Mom," she effused.

"I'm so glad to hear that," I sighed with relief. "Because to be honest, I always get a little nervous when girls your age socialize in groups."

"How come?"

"Sometimes they can fight and bicker with each other, and feelings can get hurt. I don't know why. Once girls are grown up it isn't usually that way, but I remember things like that from when I was your age."

"Umm . . . Mom?"

"Yes?"

"Actually, since you brought it up, there was something that happened."

I leaned back and listened to her story. One of the girls in the group was older than the rest. And during the afternoon, Saoirse found herself in a game with her in the tent. The older girl would zip up the windows in the tent, and Saoirse would unzip them before she could finish.

"I was having fun and we were laughing," Saoirse told me. "I don't know what I did, but suddenly she got right in front of me, right in my face, and said 'MOVE OUT OF MY WAY!'"

"I don't know why," Saoirse went on, "but it was the way she said it. It wasn't friendly at all. So I told her 'no.'" I waited for her to continue. "And then she asked me if I wanted to die. As a joke, I pretended to give it some thought, and then I said 'umm, not particularly.' Then she told me to move again, and I wouldn't do it. She pushed me, and told me that if I didn't do what she said, she'd pull my hair. Well, I figured that Ula had pulled my hair lots of times, so I told her to go ahead and do it. So she yanked it. Really hard."

"What did you do?"

"Nothing. I eventually moved. It was all kind of weird. But there was no sense in making a big deal out of it."

That's not how I felt. I wanted to call my friend, the mother who had hosted the party, and find out about who this other child was. I wanted to take measures to make sure that these two never saw each other again. Then, the pugilist in me came out.

"You just moved out of her way?"

"Yeah." I don't know what, exactly, I was hoping she'd say—that she'd decked this brat, maybe pushed her up against the wall of the tent and told her to mind her manners in a menacing tone that let her know my kid wasn't going to take any crap. But I silenced my inner beast.

"I'm not happy that happened," was all I could think to offer.

"Actually, Mom, this is going to sound kind of weird, but, umm, I kind of liked it."

"You what?!" I found this comment extremely disturbing.

"Well, it's just that—" Saoirse paused for a moment and searched for her words. "It's just that I realized I wasn't scared after all. I always figured that if something like that happened, I would be. And I wasn't. Not at all. And that just feels, well, *good*. I realized there wasn't anything she could really do to me. So it didn't bother me to back down. I mean, it was a birthday party, after all. I didn't need to ruin it."

It is at times like this when I am thankful that my children are better at acting like grown ups than their mother. While I wasn't on hand to judge who was in the wrong to begin with, in the end, Saoirse did the right thing. She backed down at her best friend's birthday party, avoiding more conflict and embarrassment for everyone.

But what struck me most was the glow around Saoirse as she told the story. She hadn't hurt anyone. But she had recognized that she could be strong in her own way, that she didn't need to be fearful of another kid pushing her around. I was reminded of a story I once read about a champion fighter who climbed onto a city bus one night with his friend after an evening out. A short way into the ride, a belligerent drunk came on board. Seeking someone to harass, he began insulting and pushing the fighter, unaware of the man's background. The fighter did nothing. He ignored the drunk, who eventually lost interest and settled down. When they got off the bus, the friend said, "You're a champion fighter. Why did you put up with that?"

And he replied, "I put up with that *because* I'm a champion fighter."

When we know our strength, it becomes less necessary to show it. Saoirse recognized that the other girl, who was acting menacing, really couldn't do much to trouble her. She walked away from the incident more aware of her own personal strength. And as she sat with me over lunch, she radiated joy at her discovery.

This has become her story. Ula asks her to retell it over and over again. And each time she does, I see an important idea enter more deeply into her consciousness: *I do not have to be afraid.* She appears to bear no resentment toward the older girl whatsoever. She talks about the fun they had at the party, and says only kind things about all the kids.

As a parent and a former teacher, I am too keenly aware of the dangers of bullying. But as a former kid, I see how overcoming it contributed positively to my own self-esteem. And I can see how enduring this bout has done the same for Saoirse. I guess I'd have to admit that a little childhood conflict here and there can be a good thing. The trouble arises when the stakes are higher, where more coercive weapons and means are involved than pulling a little hair or clobbering someone with a lunch pail.

In the end, as I consider these conflicting ideas in the balance, I know that my protective nature as a parent will ultimately win out. I will naturally seek to prevent these types of interactions from happening to my kids. But I am reminded this week of how my efforts to protect my girls will only go so far. Sooner or later, they find themselves on their own, confronting any and all circumstances that I have tried to shelter them from. I can only hope they will prevail in their hearts and souls the way Saoirse did, that they will discover their own inner power. I feel quite proud of my little girl this week.

EDITORIAL NOTE: While the term is often applied loosely, the formal definition of bullying is

> . . . unwanted, aggressive behavior among school-aged children that involves a real or perceived power imbalance. The behavior is repeated, or has the potential to be repeated, over time. Bullying includes actions such as making threats, spreading rumors, attacking someone physically or verbally, and excluding someone from a group on purpose.

To learn more, visit www.stopbullying.gov.

Reclaiming Christmas,
Radical Homemaker Style

I signed online to read my email this morning, and there, at the top of the list, was a very sensitive, careful email from my Aunt Katie. She was broaching the ever-delicate subject of Christmas presents for Saoirse and Ula. What is acceptable this year? USA-made? Eco-friendly? We will be allowing gifts, yes? And, can we please make some time to talk about the holiday menu and what foods will be allowed?

Here's the bitter truth. I've become my family's biggest pain in the ass every Christmas. Most radical homemakers probably are. We want to honor the earth and her inhabitants in our daily and holiday choices, to create quiet time for reflection and gratitude, to encourage generosity in our children (as opposed to the greed of gift-receiving). And, more likely than not, we adhere to dreadfully annoying dietary regimes that drive our relatives insane: gluten-free, local foods preferred, no refined sugars, vegetarian fare, no processed foods, only organic and grassfed meats, dairy-free—the list is endless and (admittedly) ever-changing. We're sick of the consumerism, we're sick of feeling sick after all the "well-it's-Christmas" crappy treats, we're sick of being pushed around with our kids in an endless stream of command visits and activities, we're sick of the over-stimulation wrought by endless, ecologically rapacious, quickly broken toys.

From the time Bob and I began our radical homemaking path, Christmas has been a touchy subject. The worst Christmas ever ended, 7 years ago, with my mother standing six inches from my face screaming "SCROOGE!" at the top of her lungs while tears of frustration poured down her face. I held baby Saoirse close to my body in an effort to protect her from the toxicity of a typical American holiday. The best Christmas was last year, when Bob and I woke up with a stomach bug on Christmas Eve, and my extended family whisked Saoirse and Ula away from our treeside, eco-friendly vomitorium to have a holiday while we barfed in peace and watched foreign movies.

This year, we're changing things. Again. We're directing relatives who feel duty-bound to give our kids presents from a pre-approved, inexpensive gift suggestions list; we're advocating for all away-from-home holiday meals to be potlucks so that our quirky food choices won't interfere with other friends' and relatives' celebrations. We're paring back our schedule so that we are not out of the house more than once or twice per week over the season. We've hand-made candles with the kids from our beef tallow and beeswax so that we can have our own Yule altar, complete with 12 days of quiet family-only ceremonies to honor the change in light, express gratitude for the closing year's good fortune, and make well-wishes for the year ahead. And this year, for the first time, Bob and I are making gifts to ourselves. While the days are short and the nights are long, we are indulging our desires to learn new things we've always wanted to know. Bob is teaching himself DADGAD tuning on the guitar and practicing jazz chords to accompany the girls' favorite Christmas songs. I'm finally learning how to properly work my sewing machine and teaching myself how to cable-knit.

Since we embarked on our path 12 years ago, every Christmas has been different as we've experimented with new ideas for traditions that fit the kind of holiday we want to celebrate. That can be pretty unnerving for a family that reveres never-changing holiday rituals. But over the twelve years we've been on this path, our extended family has gotten used to us. Our evolving holiday experiments have become a tradition of their own. If Christmas is supposed to be about surprises, then perhaps our perpetual change-in-traditions might be considered a special annual family surprise in their own rite.

Thankfully, our relatives understand that we are committed to our own, alternative life path, and they have made room for our perpetual efforts to reclaim the Christmas season for our own family and ideals. As for Bob and me, we acknowledge that we can't simply dismiss the holidays altogether. We need to find balance, and try again each year to find ways to make the holidays work for us *and* our relatives. After all, I don't think we could hide away beside a treeside vomitorium *every* year.

The Gift of Memories

We were just finishing up a lunch of Thanksgiving leftovers two weeks ago, when the phone rang. I picked it up to be greeted by an acquaintance of mine, Jane, who volunteers at another grassfed livestock farm about 30 minutes from here.

"Shannon, I'm calling you because I wanted to let you know that we just made the tallow soap recipe from your new cookbook," she explained quickly. I winced and tangled myself in the phone cord as I reached for my own kitchen copy of the new book, and frantically rifled through the pages in search of the recipe. Had I left something out? Was there an error we didn't catch in the proofreading and recipe testing?

"What happened?" I asked, preparing for the worst.

"Oh? The soap? That was great . . . But I wanted to tell you about what happened *after*."

Breathing a sigh of relief, I settled in on a stool to listen to Jane's story.

She began telling me about her grandmother, and explained that this woman had raised her family in the country, but died tragically at an early age. Jane's own mother had been so traumatized by the event that she rarely spoke about her childhood. As a result, Jane knows very little about her family's roots.

Jane's mother is now in her late eighties and still rather taciturn in nature, but Jane makes a point of calling her every day in an ongoing effort to stay connected. Their conversations extend to the matters of the day, Jane explained, and rarely go deeper . . . until the day she mentioned that she and her friends were rendering animal fats to make soap. Quite unexpectedly, her mother began to talk. Triggered by the memories of harvesting animals in the fall and her own mother's rendering pot, the elderly woman began sharing snippets of her memories about this process, giving Jane a rare glimpse into a family history that she'd craved all her life to hear.

I had been in a rather glum "writer's mood" that morning (I'm prone to them occasionally—bouts of panic that suddenly everyone will find my writing horrible or irrelevant, that our family will somehow be cast into the streets because I wrote a bad book, followed by despair that my books are selling too few copies, which is followed by despair that my books are selling more copies than I can afford to print, followed by despair and panic that I won't be able to write another book . . . and why should I? They give me such misery . . . You get the point.). Jane's phone call was enough to help me step outside my self-centered misery and re-join life, and I felt thankful to her. But truthfully, I thought little more about the phone call.

. . . Until a few days ago, when an email with a Word attachment landed in my inbox. It had been circulating through my Dad's side of the family, and he'd forwarded it along to my brother and me with the simple note of "Please read. Love, Dad."

I opened the document to discover that it was written by my Uncle Bill, whose wife, my Aunt Eileen, had lost a fierce battle with cancer a year and a half ago. That branch of the family is centered out of Ohio, and I've had very little contact with them growing up, so I was curious why my Dad had seen fit to send me this document, which was a personal account of my Uncle Bill's memories of Aunt Eileen.

In all the years I've known him, I've never heard Uncle Bill speak more than four or five sentences. But here before me was a 31-page recounting of his memories of his life with my aunt. He started with the very first moment he saw her red hair at a square dance at Penn State at the beginning of the 1961 fall term. From there, he narrated the details of their courtship, the ways they spent time together, their wedding, what their first apartment was like, how they lived on $185 per month. He wrote down her jokes, stories that underscored her assertive personality, the cultural clashes that occurred between my east-coast (originating in New Jersey) relatives and his Pennsylvania family (apparently we thought anything west of the NJ/PA border was wild and dangerous country). He told stories about each of their children's births, about when their house burned down, about dairy farming and growing tobacco in Ohio.

I hung on every word. And I began to understand the significance of Jane's phone call with her mother. I didn't know my Aunt Eileen very well, just as Jane had never known her grandmother. But the details of their lives—the things they thought, the way they lived, the major events in their lives, form the fabric of later generations' identities regardless.

All of us lose loved ones over the course of our lives, and the pain of those losses is especially sharp during the holiday season, when we cope with the darkness by adhering to traditions with our family and friends. And when the people who were closest to the departed can find ways to share their memories with the subsequent generations, their sharing is truly a gift—one that will not wind up in a landfill, that will not pollute the skies, that will not clutter a home, that will always fit perfectly, and will last through time. Uncle Bill's memories of Aunt Eileen are now my memories. Her jokes are my jokes. Her stories are my stories. Her lessons are my lessons. And as I raise my own children and guide them into this fast-changing world, those collected experiences will enrich our family's bank of wisdom, and become one of the sweetest gifts I've known.

Honeymoon Revival

ob and I vividly remember our first winter in the tiny house—actually, someone's weekend cabin—we'd just bought, here on the edge of this 5,000-acre state forest, high in the hills of Schoharie County. We were newly engaged; shortly thereafter, newly unemployed; and quickly following, newly broke. But stitching together a few odd jobs and business ventures made the mortgage payments manageable and we'd spend our mornings drinking coffee while I held a calculator and punched numbers, imagining different ways we could make a living. The land surrounding us was captivating. When the winter sun rose high enough in the sky, we'd head out into the cold snowy landscape, blithely unaware of the passage of time as we skied along the nearby snowmobile trails, hiked untraveled roads, snowshoed through the woods exploring the hills, ravines and streams. If we remembered, we'd bring food, perhaps some cheese in my coat pocket and a bit of wine in a bola bag. We'd do our best to return home by sunset, but it was never a worry. No one waited for us. If we wanted to eat, we would. If we wanted to skip a meal, we would. If we felt like coming home early, taking a small glass of sherry, then lying down together as the afternoon sunlight poured into our sleeping loft, that was fine, too. We'd listen to the radio, read by the wood stove, stay up as late as we chose, wake when it suited us. No one depended on us. We were on our own time, our bodies were our own, our minds free to wander wherever they were inclined.

Two years later, we were still too broke to afford our scheduled summer wedding, so before the deposits for my wedding gown, the tent rental and the outdoor furniture came due in January, we eloped on New Year's Eve, then enjoyed our January honeymoon, happily free of one more financial obligation, with plenty of beautiful snow, sparkling sunrises and vivid sunsets to round out the celebration of our union.

By the next winter, I was pregnant for Saoirse. Our winter hikes were to be shortened by bouts of nausea, our morning coffee replaced with hot milk or herbal tea, whatever my tender stomach would allow. The wine and the sherry collected dust in the basement. Within the next few years we had two beautiful daughters, with growing bodies that require regular meals, and little legs not quite suited for hours of meandering through the deep snows in our wintery landscape.

Our morning coffee is no longer about dreaming, scheming, and imagining; it is about settling squabbles among the kids, divvying up errands and negotiating our schedules. Our time outside in the woods must fit into the rigid timeline of our work and homeschool demands. Lunch must be served promptly in order to make way for afternoon activities; dinner must be served early to allow for ample story time and early bedtimes. And so it goes, round and round, that bittersweet rigidity that defines parenthood, that serves as a perpetual reminder that our bodies are somehow no longer our own.

It probably comes as no surprise, then, that when our wedding anniversary rolls around, our ideal celebration isn't to steal away to a cozy B&B, nor even to head out for a special celebratory dinner. Instead, we wait until the holidays are finished, take that first quiet weekend in January, pack the kids up, send them down to the farm with my parents, and spend the weekend on a "staycation." The car stays parked in the driveway, and we do what we want, re-living those glorious memories from our early days together.

After dropping the girls down at the farm this past weekend, we stoked up the fire and did all those things we never get to do: watched a movie (one with no talking dogs or flying horses), stayed up late talking over wine, slept late, drank coffee in bed, ate spicy food for breakfast, hiked along the snowmobile trails, spent the bulk of the day amusing ourselves with needle-felting projects, skipped lunch, went for a sunset snowshoe expedition through the woods, and came back to enjoy our supper by the fire while we listened to the radio. I knitted, and Bob played his mandolin along with the music we were hearing. Our bodies were our own again for 48 hours. We were responsible for no one but ourselves. Our conversation stretched no farther than what we might do together the next day.

And then the phone rang. Ula had a tummy ache.

And so there we were, driving down to the farm at nine o'clock that night. I felt like crying.

"We had a good day," Bob tried to reassure me as we wound along the dark and snowy roads. "At least we got that." I hunched, arms crossed, silent in my parka. "It's not the kids' fault," he added.

Ula kept her face brave when we got to the farm. "I'm okay, Mommy, really I am. I don't want to ruin your vacation." She was in her pajamas.

"She's okay," Saoirse assured me, "and, besides, *I'm* with her."

Just then, Ula smiled at me. She'd lost her front tooth earlier in the day. And as she looked up to show me, I couldn't help noticing her glassy eyes. She said she was okay. But something wasn't right.

And so we bundled the girls into the car, drove them home and put them to bed, our day of splendid honeymoon renewal suddenly a distant memory. A few hours later, Ula called me to her side. And there I sat, rubbing her back until she was able to release the contents of her stomach into a kitchen bowl. The rest of my night was spent perched on the edge of her bed, psychosomatic waves of paranoid nausea sweeping through my own body as I lay beside a vomit bowl and a little girl with notoriously bad aim. I drifted from light sleep to abrupt alertness between bouts of cleaning up puke, thinking, "right now, I really hate my job."

We made it to the pre-dawn hours when Ula began moaning and whimpering once more. "Mommy?" she whispered out into the dark.

"Here's the bowl sweetie," I jumped-to, and lifted her into position, instantly ready to catch the next one.

"I don't need to barf!" she exclaimed with exasperation.

I shifted her back into bed. "Sorry. What do you need?"

"I'm seeing shapes in the shadows. Can you just hold my hand?"

And I reached out and took her hand, and we lay there in the dark, connected. I felt my own body grow calm. It is true. My body is not my own. It is my husband's, and my children's, and there's is mine. We are a family. And maybe that Saturday was the only day Bob and I will get alone together this year. But in exchange, there is always someone's hand to hold in the dark.

It's a fair trade.

Education

Is Climate Change
a Four-Letter Word?

*S*aoirse and Ula are no strangers to four-letter words. They're growing up with farmers, for crying out loud. And no self-respecting farmer around Schoharie County is going to doll up the functions of nature with cutesy euphemisms or scientific jargon. When Saoirse was one, we tried cleaning up our language a bit, but her grandmother swears like a trucker, and her great-grandfather was adamant that such language was best learned at home, "not on the school bus!" So we gave up polite propriety. We just tell the girls "those are grown-up words. When you're old enough to know how to use them properly, you can use 'em, too."

Thus, it's rather amusing when people come to the farm and say things like, "I've got S-H-I-T on my shoes" (I do believe most reasonably intelligent children can decipher s-h-i-t). If they have linguistic slips around my children, most people are quickly apologetic, and often turn crimson with embarrassment.

Yet very few people think twice about walking into the kitchen, pulling up a chair, and saying things like, "this world is going to

H-E-double hockey sticks. If the earth's temperature rises just a few more degrees, that'll be the end of the human race!"

Okay, call me weird. I really don't care if you say "hell" in front of my children. But it seriously irks me that grown-ups don't consider the trauma they're inflicting on worried young minds by suggesting to them that their lives, and all the beautiful nature that feeds their souls, are inevitably and imminently coming to an end.

This is not to say that I am in denial about climate change. Bob and I are constantly mindful of this perilous direction. But I do not believe it is helpful to burden children with frightening facts about the state of the planet when they are largely powerless at their young age to act upon it. I can't think of a more effective way to get them to disengage from the world around them, to cut themselves off from nature, to choose apathy as an act of self defense, lest they become too attached to something that they are promised will be ripped away.

I want my children to connect to and love their natural world, to have a childhood that fills them with profound earthly joys. I can think of no better way to fuel a fire that will compel them in adulthood to heal our planet. I don't think little kids are equipped to contemplate these serious and frightening scenarios depicted with the apocalyptic flair that grown-ups find necessary for climate change discussions.

I ardently believe children should be raised with an awareness of their impact on the earth. But rather than frightening them, I seek to empower Saoirse and Ula with lifestyle skills that will enable them to help the human race adapt and evolve into a beneficent species. We teach them to pick up litter, use up leftovers, to compost. We walk in our fields with our livestock and talk about the importance of the spongy soil beneath our feet and the power of the blades of grass between our toes. We limit the number of trips in our car, we sew buttons back on their dresses, we emulate the words of Thoreau, "my greatest skill is to want but little," and we perpetually strive to cultivate that as our ultimate achievement.

I cannot cover their ears whenever a well-meaning (and justifiably angry) grown-up rages about the consequences of unsatisfactory progress in climate reparations. I wince and endure it. When the girls ask questions later on, Bob and I don't deny the problem. But then we try to direct their attention instead to what we are doing about it, and what we can do better: "That's why we grow food for our community. That's why we don't buy all those plastic toys. That's why we try not to drive so much. That's why Mommy and Daddy are writing, speaking, protesting." We emphasize that there is a better world that can come of all this, that we can adapt. If we want to see change, then we can't overwhelm and discourage the young minds who will be responsible for seeing it through.

Love is a far more powerful motivator than fear. While we cannot bleep out my friends' and neighbors' fear-inducing remarks about the climate, Bob and I can encourage Saoirse and Ula to love their planet, re-direct their attention to the powers they have to change it, and most importantly, to be part of the change ourselves . . . even if that means putting up with a little extra S-H-I-T.

Love Trumps Math

When I picture a homeschooling parent, I can't help but envision the über-caregiver; a person who is so lovingly in-tune with his or her children that their young minds effortlessly blossom like sunflowers with a superb, smiling, seamless education. Through intuition and grace, homeschooling parents help their children side-step the emotional trauma experienced by so many victims of the conventional education system.

I tried to hold that vision in my head this week as I sat on my hands to avoid shaking Saoirse when she couldn't grasp how to add 10 to a number in her head. We wrote out equations: 31+10=41; 57+10=67; 35+10=45. We looked at it on the abacus as we worked on the equations, and within minutes she was writing down equations all on her own. Then, I handed her a worksheet with a list of numbers to which she was supposed to add 10. First she added 1 to everything. Then she added 11. Then 100. I put the abacus back in front of her.

"Try it on this again."

"No."

"But if you see it again, you'll understand the pattern."

"No. I hate the stupid abacus. It's stupid. Stupid." (Note to self: we MUST learn synonyms for *stupid*.)

"Then how would you like to complete the problems?"

"I can do it in my head." And so she'd erase everything furiously, then stare blankly at the page before she went back to adding 1 or 100 arbitrarily to each number.

"Saoirse, you're doing it wrong. Again. Try the abacus."

And around and around we went, getting progressively louder, the worksheet growing more wrinkled, torn and damp with eraser marks and tears; while I developed this hateful reproachful tone in my voice that suggested she was GOING to use that damn abacus, not because it was a helpful tool, but because I'm the MAMA, and I'm the ALPHA, and that's the way it's going to be. PERIOD.

During those moments, I thought about public school teachers, and decided that they deserved every penny they earn. I wanted to slam down my book and declare, "if you won't learn from me, then go to public school and see if you like it better!"

But I didn't. However, I didn't keep a calm, sweet voice, either. It's just not in my nature. "Why do you hate the abacus? Because you think it's cheating?"

Crying, she nodded.

"It's not cheating!" I jumped up, ran to my desk, then came back to the table with my calculator. "Here. This is a calculator." I showed her how to punch in the numbers to get the result. I watched her glee at how easy the answer came, then spewed the venom. "Doing that kind of math on a calculator is cheating! It doesn't help you think! It doesn't help you see what is happening. The abacus is a TOOL. When you get confused, it helps you to picture what you need to do. You can't learn it if you can't see it!"

"I'm not going to use ANY of it!" She screamed back at me and pushed the calculator and abacus across the table.

"Saoirse! You have such high expectations of yourself, but you won't allow yourself to go through the process of achieving them. You want to be good at math, and you are, but you can't simply *know* everything without going through a learning process first!" Yes. It did occur to me that this babble was going right over her head. But I couldn't stop myself.

Meanwhile, I was hating myself. I closed the books, told her we couldn't go on for the day. She ran upstairs and flung herself on her bed, crying. I went and sat in my rocking chair and engaged in a robust session of self-loathing. If I was a good homeschooling mom, I would see the flaw in the curriculum. I would love my kid so much that I'd never hurt her feelings while trying to teach her. I could sit in this rocking chair and acknowledge that SHE wasn't to blame. *I* was. It was *my* fault. I'd recover my calm, sweetly apologize, hug her, and we'd move forward.

But I couldn't. All I could do was think about all her personal failings, and how *I* was right and *she* was wrong.

I stood up and slammed lunch onto the table. I curtly called everyone to eat. I didn't bother with her when she wouldn't come downstairs. A few minutes later, she came to the table. We wouldn't look at each other. I stared straight ahead and chewed my meatloaf. Someone knocked at the door, and Bob went to see who it was. Ula ran after him, leaving the two of us together.

I kept staring straight ahead, thinking: *School teachers know how to deal with this. I don't. I should just give up and enroll her. But I can't. It would break her heart. She loves being here with me. Why can't she allow herself to be imperfect and then experience the learning she needs to reach her goal? Why can't I be a better homeschooling parent?*

Why am I sitting here, not talking to my kid, and being a jerk? Is this what she's going to learn about how we deal with conflict?

Before I could think better of it, I turned, still with tension in my voice, and forced myself to say my truth. Looking her in the eyes, I said,

"Saoirse. I love you. And I don't care if you never do math. I'll always love you." I wasn't ready to apologize yet, even if a better über-caring homeschooling parent would have. I wasn't ready to let her off the hook, probably because I wasn't ready to let myself off the hook for being a jerk homeschooling parent.

She didn't say anything, but I watched her shoulders relax. We remained silent. I think we were too lost in our thoughts. We are so very much alike. She didn't want the humiliation of the abacus, because she was ashamed that she couldn't meet her own expectations in math. I didn't want the humiliation of apologizing, because I couldn't meet my own expectations as a homeschooling parent. We both had a lot to think about, but at least the anger was gone.

I left the table and went into my office to work. A few minutes later, she was at my side. "Mommy? I'm sorry about the abacus."

I looked up at her. "You are?"

She nodded.

It was my turn. "I was a jerk. I'm sorry, too." She threw her arms around me. "I don't really know what I'm doing," I added. " I'm just trying the best I can with this homeschooling thing."

"I know."

"I think the problem wasn't the abacus. I think the worksheet didn't make sense to you. Because you knew how to do the math when the worksheet wasn't there."

"I think you're right."

"What should we do about the abacus?"

"I think I'll try every math problem in my head first. Then I'll use the abacus if I'm not getting it."

"And we can throw out that worksheet," I suggested.

She nodded. "Good idea . . . It's . . . "

" . . . stupid," we both concluded.

So here we are, at the dawn of another homeschool day, two deeply imperfect souls trying to figure out how to learn together. It was naive of me to think that, by schooling my child at home, I could spare her from emotional injury. Life is a minefield of emotional injuries, just waiting to happen, no matter what educational path we're on. This week, the most important lesson we can both glean is figuring out how to forgive each other, and ourselves, and then move on with the learning.

Summer Walks with
(or without) Santa Claus

*S*aoirse is now at the age where we can take long walks together. She no longer insists on carrying her Froggy, or her favorite doll, Lily; she doesn't require that I pack a picnic feast to fuel her energy for the return journey, nor does she need to stop and rest every 3 minutes as we ascend a hill.

And as it was with me and my mom, we now have our time for girl talk, to leisurely explore all things of interest to girls her age, to recount adventures and share secrets, safe from the interruptions of little sisters, ringing telephones or the general demands of the day. While out padding down our road listening to crickets and robins, I find myself opening up and exploring my inner thoughts with her in a way that simply isn't possible around our chaotic kitchen table. Neither of us has any particular agenda. We just share what comes to mind.

The other day, for me, it was Santa Claus.

"Saoirse," I began, "there's something important I need to tell you."

"What is it, Mom?"

I sighed. "There's no such thing as Santa Claus." She walked along silently, saying nothing. I blathered on. "It's just that, well, you're spending time with more and more kids these days, and sooner or later, one of them is going to tell you that Santa Claus isn't real—that grown-ups invented him."

She looked very confused. The summer sun was beating down on the road. It was hardly a time for talking about Christmas, but there it was. I'd come clean. I waited for her response.

"So . . ." she proceeded slowly, choosing her words with care, "what . . . happens at Christmas now?"

Oops. Silly me. I neglected the pragmatic matters that would occupy any kid's mind first and foremost. "You still get presents," I quickly assured her. She breathed a sigh of relief. Then, with a bit of venomous vindication directed toward that right jolly old elf, I added, "But they come from your father and me. We do all the hard work to make Christmas nice. And quite frankly, it's very exhausting running around trying to make it look like it's some big fat guy who comes down a chimney."

There. I'd said it. I waited for her next reaction. After a few moments she said, "Then, now that I know, can I help you and Dad make Christmas for Ula?"

It hadn't occurred to me that this Santa confession could have the added advantage of expanding the elf workforce.

"Yes! Absolutely! . . . And Saoirse?"

"Yes?"

"While I'm at it, the Easter Bunny? Giant rabbit that messes up the house by dumping eggs all over? Doesn't exist, either."

"I was wondering about that."

"And about the Tooth Fairy?"

"Yes?" She looked at me in alarm, but I was on a roll.

"If you give me the tooth and I promise to give you cash, can we just agree that I don't have to wake up in the middle of the night to shove it under your pillow?"

"Mom!" She exclaimed, "Why are you telling me all this?"

Upholding cultural myths can grow tiresome for parents. Prattling on to our kids, pretending to believe things we don't may seem charming at first, but after a while, it makes me feel like a liar. But that's not the full reason for my disclosure. My heart was open, and there was no closing it at this point.

"Because there is *real* magic in this world, Saoirse," I rushed on, tears coming to my eyes as I went on, "and I'm afraid that if you believe that things like Santa Claus, the Easter Bunny and the Tooth Fairy are real because I told you, and then someone else tells you that they aren't, that you'll think the other things we believe aren't real, either."

As I reflect back on that morning, that conversation wasn't really about Santa. It was about faith, and my fear that my child may someday lose it. We don't ascribe to any single religion in our home. We believe in many things—in a great oneness, in the wisdom of Jesus, the teachings of Buddha. We explore the Greek, Roman, Celtic, and Egyptian gods, work with healers, create altars to nature, make time to honor the spirits of the dead, drink elderflower tea and sing in the woods to bring out the fairies on midsummer night. I cannot find it in my heart to rule out any spiritual possibility. As I have grown up in this world, faith has kept my life full of wonder, inspiration and possibility. And as I watch Saoirse grow up and begin to engage with the world beyond my reach, I feel compelled to do everything I can to keep the magic of faith alive for her. But the truth is that only *she* can keep that alive within herself. The best I can do, as I watch this child grow into her own, is to live my own life with sincerity, and lay myself open to her, take as many walks with her as I can, and stop hiding my reverence for this world behind the façade of Santa Claus and the Easter Bunny.

We didn't discuss this any further that day. But about a week later, we were up at the farm pond for an afternoon swim. "Mom? Can we have some time to talk?"

"Sure." We swam out of the water to a nearby rock and perched ourselves in the sun to dry. I waited for her to speak.

"It's about Lily. I needed to talk to you while she wasn't around." Indeed, the doll was safe from earshot, back on Saoirse's bed at home.

"What about Lily?"

"Do you think I should tell her the truth about Santa Claus?" I carefully considered her question.

"I think you need to answer that question for yourself, Saoirse. But whatever you do, stay true to your heart." I had to smile to myself. Maybe Santa Claus had been exposed as a fraud. But imagination was still a powerful part of Saoirse's personal magic.

My Kids Have Something To Say

*S*aoirse was no more than a few weeks old when one of our farm customers approached me about attending a protest in Albany to call legislators' attention to the problems with genetically modified foods. The organizers were specifically recruiting mothers to attend with their children. They wanted moms to put kids and babies in shopping carts and wheel them from office to office to call attention to the cause. I wholeheartedly agreed with my customer about the importance of the issue. But I immediately refused.

"I'm not using my child as a decoration for a cause she hasn't chosen," was the only thing I could think to say.

Later on, upon recounting the experience with Bob, he agreed. Our refusal to use our children as a contrivance for our causes became a household rule for many reasons. But Saoirse, now nine, and Ula, six, recently informed us that they've outgrown that rule.

First, to explain Bob's and my thinking: We believe that to raise a child who will be a good steward of the earth, she must be allowed to fall in love with it. We felt that bombarding our kids with information about our causes—how the earth is being poisoned and abused— before they are empowered to take action to protect it is problematic.

If the natural world were forever depicted to them as fragile, in danger, and in need of protection, they might simply detach from it, since they were powerless to do anything about it. We wanted our children to grow to trust the earth, to feel nurtured by her, before they were asked to defend her.

Rather than barraging them with stories about what others are doing wrong to this planet, we tried to make them aware of the things that we all must do to treat her right, whether it is picking up trash on the side of the road, being careful with our water and streams on the farm, choosing local foods in season, assiduously composting and recycling, or minimizing our use of our car. Furthermore, there was the simple matter of our daughters being too young to have opinions on issues. How does an infant or young child have an opinion about GMOs? Organic food policy? The 99 percent? New York State environmental law? Over the course of our family life, Bob and/or I would leave home to speak out for our causes, and the kids would stay home. The girls, now 6 and 9 years old, never challenged that rule, until last week.

As the threat of hydraulic fracturing circles about New York State, an unprecedented number of the residents of our town from all backgrounds and across the political spectrum have decided to organize to get a law in place to protect our land. And while it would appear that no one on our town board is truly "pro-fracking," the speed with which the citizens want to enact the law is deeply troubling for the board members, who are accustomed to taking 6-12 months to discuss something as minor as a single dog-control incident. A new law on the books would preferably be a multi-year process in their view. This is one of those towns where nothing is supposed to happen, where the greatest controversy is over tax assessments. But the citizens feel it is imperative to have a town law in place now, before the state makes its determination on whether to permit drilling. Many of us feel "home rule" is our best chance for protecting ourselves in the future. Thus, while it would seem most folks are in agreement on the issues, there is still controversy.

And Saoirse and Ula hear it. The topic comes up at our local parties and potlucks, they hear about it at community meetings at the firehouse, when we run into neighbors at the post office, when we go to vote at the town barn, when neighbors drop their kids off for play dates, or when folks come by the farm to purchase meat.

On the day of our public hearing for the proposed law last week, Saoirse and Ula sat down at lunch while Bob and I were reviewing our talking points. They waited for a lapse in our conversation, then Saoirse spoke up. "I'd like to talk tonight."

"Me, too," chimed in Ula.

I stammered. Saoirse? Speak? This is a kid who can go weeks without seeing any of her buddies and be perfectly happy in her seclusion. She is friendly to everyone she meets, but she's an introvert to the core. And Ula? She's usually playing in her fantasy world; what does she know about the issues?

"This isn't your problem," I assured them. "Mommy and Daddy will deal with it."

Saoirse emitted a perfectly executed pre-adolescent gasp of exasperation (she's been practicing them a lot lately).

"It is SO our problem! We want to be able to live here! We want to be able to drink the water!"

Bob and I stared at each other. What to do?

"I don't think it's allowed," I muttered.

"You're not of voting age," he added, then quickly changed the subject. "Ula, make sure you eat your vegetables."

"Saoirse, can you pass me the butter?" I aided the direction-change.

The afternoon passed with nothing more said on the subject. The girls went about finishing their lessons and playing, and we assumed it was forgotten . . . until just before supper, when they marched in to where we were having tea.

"You need to help us prepare what we're going to say tonight," Saoirse informed us.

Bob and I stuttered and stammered some more.

"You're serious?" I finally asked. "You don't have to do this."

"I HAVE to say something," Saoirse informed me. "I just HAVE to."

So we booted up the computer, and Saoirse drafted a simple statement in her own words. Ula dictated what she wanted to say. We encouraged her to keep it short, since she wouldn't be able to read any notes.

When we arrived at the town meeting, their names were added to the list of speakers. They shared speakers' turn #17.

I was sitting behind them when their names were called in that packed room. They stood up. Saoirse held her paper in front of her. Her hands didn't even shake. Ula stood beside her, staring over her spectacles at each board member at the head of the room, daring them to avert her gaze.

"My name is Saoirse Hayes Hooper," Saoirse began, "and this is my sister, Ula. We live on Rossman Valley Road, and we work on Sap Bush Hollow Farm with our grandparents. The reason we don't want fracking is because we have a very happy and healthy family, and we want it to stay that way. We want for our family to be able to drink a glass of water without having to worry about getting sick. So my sister and I are asking you to please BAN FRACKING."

And then, Ula added her one line, "We don't want Mother Earth to be in pain all the time."

"Thank you," they managed to say in unison.

They both collapsed into my lap afterward.

I don't know what the board members thought. Did they believe that I'd brought my children out as decorations for the cause? Did they feel I had manipulated them to say something to bring more drama to the scene? Just then, Saoirse leaned in and whispered in my ear, "I'm so happy to finally get that off my chest."

And I realized that my concerns were pointless. It didn't matter what the board, or any of my neighbors thought about a nine-year-old and a six-year-old standing up and speaking out at a public hearing. It didn't matter whether or not anyone suspected that I was some kind of manipulative over-bearing mother pushing these girls to do my bidding. Saoirse and Ula needed to do this for themselves. They needed to know that they had taken a stand on something that was important to them.

I understand now how Bob's and my job as parents is shifting. It is not necessarily our task any longer to shield our daughters from our grown-up causes and concerns. We still don't feel it is appropriate to ask them to stand up for issues that don't resonate with them, nor should they have the joy they take from living on this earth stripped away by incessant harping about all the problems we must battle. But at the same time, we can't silence them, either. They have grown to love their world, and even at their young age, they have every right to defend it. Our job now is to help them make their voices heard.

The Redo

*S*aoirse gaped at me in horror this past fall when she submitted her first written school report, and I returned it to her with penciled-in notes scratched about the pages, along with instructions to re-write it.

I assured her that the work was good, but the next step in the writing process was to make it *great*. Her mouth opened and closed like a fish as she tried to think what to say, staring at those marks that marred her work.

Then she picked up an eraser, and began erasing her errors, along with my comments, then writing in her corrections.

"No," I told her firmly. "You need to re-write."

This brought on tears of frustration and shame for her. It brought on a serious case of self-doubt for me.

The hardest subject for me to teach my kids is writing. I thought it would be the easiest, owing to the fact that such a large part of my livelihood, and my life's joy, is derived from this particular craft. It turns out the opposite is true. I care so much about the subject, I feel as though I have no gauge on what constitutes "good" work for a child her age. And I want so dearly for her to love and feel empowered by writing, that I find myself blinded with fear at the thought that she'll hate it on account of my instruction.

And here I was, criticizing her work, and assigning her something that seemed like busy-work—the arduous, unfulfilling task of writing a second draft of a perfectly adequate report.

In my own work, I have the luxury of a word processing program. Edits are easy. Highlight, delete, re-type only those parts that don't work. Spell-check handles a lot of the type-errors. The printer spits out a new draft instantly.

But I won't let Saoirse use the computer yet. I feel that she needs to develop a grasp of good, efficient penmanship before she learns keyboard skills. I feel like she needs to understand writing intimately, as a union between her mind and her hands, before she lets a computer interfere with her process.

But what of her idea—to simply use the eraser and squeeze in her corrections? In hindsight, I admit that it perhaps seemed reasonable, but I wouldn't give in. I didn't have solid reasons at that time, only a gut instinct that somehow, as in my own learning process, re-drafting by hand was critical to my development as a writer. I wouldn't cave, although I had serious misgivings.

I didn't abandon her completely to the labor. I stayed in the room with her as she worked, hoping my presence would calm her and enable her to focus. I picked up my knitting. It was a new project. Late last fall I decided to teach myself Fair Isle knitting, and my newest endeavor at that time was to knit an over-sized sweater for Saoirse, using colors she'd chosen.

That sweater accompanied me through a lot of Saoirse's re-write projects that fall and winter. She continued to fight my insistence on the process, but the arguments got progressively shorter as she realized that I wasn't changing my position. She also seemed glad to see me chipping away at the sweater that she was eager to have. As I worked, she'd periodically walk over and pet the wool, running her hands over the knit patterns with a smile on her face. It did seem to work as a salve for us both.

Incidentally, as her arguments about re-drafting grew shorter and shorter, the sleeves on Saoirse's sweater grew longer and longer.

I finished knitting it two weeks ago, and proudly placed it in her lap one morning when she came down for breakfast. She beamed at me, and quickly pulled it on over her pajamas. The sleeves were, indeed, a bit of a problem, falling well below her extended thumbs. I grabbed the sweater and quickly folded back the cuffs. The arms still fell below her thumbs. I folded them again. And again. There. *Now* the length was right . . . although she had two inches of extra wool circling in a wad at the top of her hands.

"The sweater was supposed to be over-sized," I reminded her.

Saoirse is a deeply thoughtful girl. She struggles to say anything that would ever hurt my feelings. This time was no exception. She just nodded and smiled at me weakly. In spite of the smile, she was unable to hide the disappointment. The sweater had been something she'd been dreaming about for some time . . . and she hadn't envisioned it quite like . . . *this*.

"You're growing so fast, you'll be glad to have those extra-long sleeves in a couple years," I tried again. She nodded. Then she became enthusiastic.

"You're right, Mom. I can just put it away until then!"

Oh, crap. I could read the subtext in that one. I stared at her.

"Turn around." I grabbed my pincushion, unrolled the sleeves and began experimenting with ways to shorten it. Perhaps I could sew along the seams where the sleeves joined the body, taking off a few inches and hiding them beneath the sweater, only to be let out later? I thought about the big bulky cuff that would rub her arm. No. That wouldn't work. I stared at her.

And then I thought about all that knitting I'd done while she was re-writing her papers for me. What was I teaching if I didn't show the same commitment to re-doing my own work, when I expected it of her?

"I know what to do," I finally concluded.

"You can fix it?" Her eyes brightened.

"Yup. I'm going to take the sweater apart, unravel all the extra length on the sleeves, then put it back together again."

"No!" Saoirse began to cry. "I can't let you do that! Not after all the work you put in!"

I took her in my arms, and we snuggled down into a chair together.

"Sweetie," I said, kissing the top of her head, "If I don't re-do my work, then all of it will be wasted, because the sweater will be useless to you."

"I'll wear it! I promise! Just like it is! Don't un-do all that work! The sweater is beautiful!"

And here, in this pile of knitting, was my chance to finally give a good writing lesson. "But it's not right. It can be better. And I know how to fix it, so I will. It's just a little more time. Give me back the sweater."

She hugged herself and kept the sweater away, crying at the thought that she would reject something I'd made for her, that she'd send me back for a re-do.

"Saoirse. Look at me." Her wet eyes met mine.

"Do I make you re-write your essays and reports?"

"Yes."

"Then I can re-make your sweater."

She thought about it for a moment, then took the sweater off. Two days later, she had a new sweater, with sleeves that were a perfect length.

A few days after that, while I was giving a knitting lesson to a friend, Saoirse joined us in the living room and began a new project of her own, a knitted headband. Still awkward with her needles, she dropped a stitch here, picked it up a little later, and had a piece of knitting at the end of two hours that was 80 percent glorious.

"What do you think?" She asked me.

"Well," I looked over her work. "Can you see what happened over here?"

"I dropped a stitch," she admitted. "But I fixed it later, see?"

"But that makes it wobbly. Is that what you want?"

"Are you telling me I have to pull it out?"

"Absolutely not. This is your project. If it were mine, I'd pull it out, because I'd want my headband to be just right. But this is your headband, and if you like it the way it is, then that's your choice. All that matters is that you like it."

She stared at her work for a few moments, then yanked out her needle and began to unravel the wool. At the end of the day, she came to me, beaming, with a perfectly knit headband.

A simple re-do. And there's the greater lesson, bigger than writing, bigger than knitting.

I feel very strongly that my children's happy future is not tied to how well they behave, or whether or not they are able to hold a job. It is tied to their ability to create with their minds and their hands. They might be making something that they need for themselves, they might be making something that they will gift, sell or trade. And while I don't hope to engender paralyzing perfectionism, I still want to impart that the key to taking pleasure from such a life is that their work will meet their own expectations, that they can have a vision in their imagination, then bring it to fruition. And if that doesn't happen the first time, what matters even more is that they are confident enough in their skills, in their ability to continuously learn, and familiar enough with the process of creation, to know that they can always re-do it, and make it even better.

And so, in the teaching of this lesson, I am forced to learn it myself.

Sex Ed

*S*aoirse pitched a bit of a fit a few months ago when Bob and I dropped her and Ula off down at the farm with my parents. We were going home for a date night. She had a few creative works in progress on her craft table, she knew we were having lobster for dinner, we were at a good part in the book we were reading at bedtime, and she just didn't want to be separated from her mommy.

I didn't give in. I give enough hours to my children in the day and in the night that I tend to suffer little remorse or guilt when I hand them off in order to get some time alone with Bob. But upon leaving her behind, and her weeping and acting as though I was abandoning her in the streets, I decided she was old enough for me to experiment with offering a more thorough explanation for my actions.

So the next night, after she returned home and was perched on the kitchen stool across from me as I made supper, happily chatting away, I made my move.

"Saoirse," I said, leaning across the counter, "we need to talk about something."

"What?"

"About my leaving you down at the farm last night."

"What about it?"

"I wanted to go home and have time with . . . have *sex* with your father."

Her jaw dropped open and she seemed incapable of a response. I was acting from my gut on this one, and I needed to charge forward before I lost my courage.

"Look, it's like this. Parents who love each other have sex with each other." She gave me the grossed-out kid look. "Oh, quit acting surprised. You know your dad and I have sex. If we never did, you wouldn't be here. That's part of what makes a happy marriage." As an afterthought I added, "And a happy marriage means that you kids get a happy family life."

Her mouth closed and she nodded. I took that as a cue that I could fumble ahead.

"And I'm madly in love with you and your sister. I love all the time I spend with you. But other parents send their kids off to school, and in other families, the kids sleep in separate bedrooms. Your dad and I don't make you sleep in a separate bedroom (we have a large loft that functions as a "family bedroom" in our house—for now, anyway . . .), and I don't send you away to school every day. And while that means your dad and I get to spend a lot of great time with you, we also need time alone once in a while, to take care of our marriage."

"It's okay, mom, I get it," she said, with a tone of finality. "But you made sure you won't get pregnant, right?"

This. From a nine-year-old.

Clearly, the discussion of preventing conception is not a new topic for her. While I had never, until this moment, admitted to a time and date for the actual crime, I never denied that her dad and I have a sex life, either. A set of cycle beads hangs from my bedside reading lamp that Saoirse and Ula have thoroughly explored and asked questions about; they've seen a box of condoms in the bathroom drawer ("Is this gum?" Ula asked hopefully); we've talked about how pregnancy happens; when it happens; the different options for contraception; the rationale behind Bob's and my particular choices. I never sat down to give them any formal lectures on the topic. I simply decided early on that I wasn't going to shy away from the questions they asked. As they get older, their questions get more sophisticated, and so do my answers. I want them to be comfortable enough with their sexuality to be able to wait until the time is right. In my deepest hopes, the right time for sexual intercourse will be once they have entered into a monogamous relationship, when a pregnancy, even if unintended, can be supported appropriately. But no matter what, I believe the best way to teach sexual education is to model a healthy, happy union.

Our daughters' sexual education is a family matter. In our household, we resist the use of conventional drugs. We resist buying GMO foods or food that has been treated with chemical fertilizers, pesticides, antibiotics or hormones. We treat our family's routine illnesses with herbs, reiki, massage, chiropractic care, kinesiology, and homeopathic medicines before we will allow any form of conventional medical intervention. Thus, we hope they can make similar holistic choices about their bodies when they become sexually active. And the key to making a holistic choice that honors their bodies and spirits, is information.

No matter the choices they make about their sexuality, Bob and I want to be the first people they turn to when they have questions or concerns. As such, we need to make sure the door is open for them to ask any and all questions. Even though the tips of his ears visibly burn red, Bob does his best to answer any questions they pose to him about penises and erections. The less abashed partner, I easily tell them anything they want to know about vaginas. And we don't hide our affection for each other. They catch us smooching in the kitchen, sigh with mock disgust when we make eyes at each other over dinner, tease us when they find us cuddled up on the couch. Living a happy life in love is the most important sexual education we can give our kids.

So there we sat, Saoirse and I, as I explained my rationale for leaving her at the farm that previous night. Our conversation was wrapping up. I was scooping kale salad out of a bowl with my hands and arranging it on the dinner plates when she leaned across the counter once more.

"Mom?"

"Yes?"

"One more thing."

"What is it, sweetie?"

"Please just tell me you washed your hands afterward."

Without a Diploma,
Does the Scarecrow Have a Brain?

*I*t was less than a week after I'd defended my Ph.D. dissertation when I sat down at my computer to complete Cornell University's online graduate placement questionnaire. Supposedly, upon answering each of the multiple-choice questions about my interests, experiences and coursework, the computer program would match me with any number of potential employers specifically in search of a Cornell grad with my unique skills and talents.

After two hours of carefully considering each response, I clicked "submit."

Three days later I received my one and only career possibility.

After receiving a Masters degree and Ph.D. from Cornell University with a 3.9 G.P.A., where I had specialized in sustainable agriculture and community development, I was singularly qualified to apply for a job writing scripts for the World Wide Wrestling Federation.

This was one of many moments when I deeply questioned the value of higher education.

This story has come to my mind often in the past few weeks, as I've had the opportunity to meet with students from four different colleges, both public and private, along the East Coast. These scholars have run the gamut from barely literate (incredible!) to brilliantly committed to finding ways to heal the earth and rebuild a sustainable economy.

While I enjoyed the opportunity to speak to a younger population about the concepts of sustainability, I found myself deeply worried about all of them. The United States Department of Education reports that the price for public university tuition rose 42 percent between 2001 and 2011, and private schools jumped 31 percent. The Chronicle of Higher Education reports that 60 percent of college students are borrowing money each year to cover their tuition. I don't think that figure includes the personal debts incurred by parents trying to help their kids pay these bills, or the drain on their savings that go toward college expenses.

This data sprung to mind this week when one student asked me how I would make education more sustainable. Naturally, I think we need to find ways to lower the costs. But as I pondered his question, I realized there was more to the problem. The prevalent axiom that typically sends kids to school is the notion that they'll earn more money with a college degree than they will with just a high school diploma. I have two concerns about this claim:

1. This assumes that students are accepting conventional employment upon leaving school. I happen to believe that if we are to rebuild a sustainable society, then we need more people to step outside the parameters of conventional employment and instead begin small businesses that operate within a life-serving economy, where everyone is able to earn a living wage, where ecological resources are sustained, where community life is vibrant, and where relationships are easily nurtured.

If a student craves employment in the global economy, where an employer will not consider them to be intelligent and competent without a college degree, then perhaps the diploma is worth buying. But while intelligence and an ability to learn are required to be in business for oneself, a diploma is *not*. Obviously, this argument doesn't carry to those folks who require professional certifications in order to be in practice, such as architects, doctors, nurses, school teachers, etc. But there are a lot of livelihoods in which professional certification isn't necessary. And while some advanced training or an apprenticeship will likely be needed in order to hang out a shingle, a college diploma may not be. And if a college diploma comes with a debt package, it may hamper the graduate's freedom to choose self-employment. That scares me. The next generation cannot help us to unravel the extractive economy and re-build a life-serving alternative if they are too indebted to avoid ecologically and socially extractive employment.

2. If college students "earn more" than non-college graduates, that also suggests that there is a bias in our society against those who choose to opt out of school. Some of the most intelligent, articulate, skilled and learned people I've come across on my life path have been drop-outs. If I could make one generalization about all of the high-achieving drop outs I've met, it is that they saw their education as their own responsibility, and they took it upon themselves to learn. Most of them described the prescriptive academic process of acquiring a formal degree as stifling. If we are going to make education more sustainable, then we need to challenge the cultural myth that intelligence is determined by a diploma. It seems our nation truly believes that the Scarecrow in the Wizard of Oz was without a brain until he was handed a diploma.

Education, in itself, is free for the taking, if one is willing to do the work. It can be found in libraries, online, through apprenticeships, from mentors, and through community and family relationships. College is a great choice for some, but it is just one of many options for acquiring an education. Just because a person has not paid for a diploma does not mean they are un-educated. As long as our society continues to buy into the myth that the diploma bestows brains, then we are agreeing to externalize and commodify both learning and intelligence, two divinely awarded gifts bestowed on every human being at birth.

This is not to say that I am not appreciative of my own years at college. They gave me a start in life that I didn't know how to invent on my own. But I've often reflected upon that time, wondering if I could have walked the same path of writing, thinking, entrepreneurship and farming, had I not earned four degrees (five, if you count high school). I think of Ben Hewitt, an accomplished writer, thinker and farmer in Vermont, who also happens to be a high school drop-out, leading a life very similar to my own. And I can't help but conclude that, yes, if I'd had a bit more imagination, I probably could have found a way. Truth be told, I was an unhappy scholar, but I was afraid to challenge convention enough to try an alternative route to learning. I envy Ben's early recognition of his ability to self-teach and find a creative path.

But of course, maybe he envies me, since I'm uniquely qualified to write scripts for the World Wide Wrestling Federation.

Neighbors

Sharing the Harvest

It is as harmless as a dove, as beautiful as a rose, and as valuable as flocks and herds. It has been longer cultivated than any other, and so is more humanized . . . for when man migrates, he carries with him not only his birds, quadrupeds, insects, vegetables, and his very sword, but his orchard also.

—Henry David Thoreau (*Wild Apples*, 1862)

f I had to choose one food whose flavor fully encapsulates the glory of fall, it would have to be the wild apple. I can close my eyes, take a bite, and know what it is to taste an autumn-blue sky accented by golden rods, deep purple asters, the lush of green pasture, and the first red leaves on the sugar maples.

Each year, Bob and I make plans with our friend Bernie for our annual fall cider pressing. Once the date is set, our job is to meander through the feral orchards gifted to us by the earliest settlers on our respective farms, sample each tree's offerings, and gather fruit. Our "pressing club" has one simple rule: No commercial apples. The best cider should capture the ethereal ambrosia surrounding an untainted orchard. That means foraging and mixing countless old varieties to balance sweet, tart and floral flavors, creating a glorious blend that honors our earliest agrarian predecessors, and nourishes us all winter long.

Trouble is, this year, there are hardly any apples to be found on our land. A late localized snowstorm that killed our blossoms and dampened our spirits at the start of the growing season haunts us yet again, thwarting our cider harvest. Bernie reports that he'll have ample apples to meet his needs for pressing. But we can hardly scare up a bushel. Our hilltop trees may have borne no fruit, but Bob and I notice apples glittering, untouched, on trees throughout the low-land community—in abandoned pastures, road sides, and forest edges. I should feel buoyed by the abundant potential harvest surrounding me, but I don't. None of the apple trees stand on land owned by people I know. In order to access them, I will have to knock, uninvited, on the doors of strangers, and request permission to gather the harvest.

I believe in the power of building community, of expanding resources and generating abundance by forging relationships. But believing something and practicing one's beliefs are two entirely different matters. I hate knocking on the doors of strangers. Upstate New York is a pretty conservative area. The cars outside the homes I must approach bear jingoistic slogans for a variety of causes to which I am dubious at best, opposed at worst. In an effort to blend in locally, our car has always been unadorned of our causes ("Actions speak louder than bumper stickers," my husband is fond of saying). But upon opening our car doors, a clutter of reusable shopping bags, apple cores, and refillable water bottles spill onto the ground around our barefooted family, belying our best efforts to "be normal."

With empty boxes in my trunk, I muster my courage and pull into the driveway of the first home where I hope to glean fruit. I knock on the door. A woman opens it partway and peers around the side. Her storm door remains closed to me. Her eyebrows are furrowed, leading me to believe that she is both annoyed and frightened by my unexpected appearance. I tell her where I live, explain my situation, and the absolute worst thing that can happen, does:

She tells me no. Politely.

Scarlet-faced from humiliation, I scurry back to the car and confront the expectant gazes of my girls, who are eager to begin picking. I tell them the bad news and watch their faces fall. Saoirse and Ula do not define winter by Christmas, nor by presents. When the first hints of the cold season hit, they practically rupture with excitement over the prospect of cider and popcorn by the fire. The idea of depriving them this simple delight outweighs my faltering courage. With confidence, I tell them that, within 24 hours, I will find enough apples for the cider pressing.

I bring them back home for lunch, leave Ula with Bob for her nap, then persuade Saoirse, presently seven, to join me on my mission. I brush her hair and wipe food off her cheeks, unabashedly taking advantage of her youthful cuteness. Any person who tells me "No" will have to say it to her adorable face. We drive to the next house on my list. We both get out, remembering this time to put some flip-flops on our feet. We are successful. Tossing the flip-flops in the back seat, we grab our boxes and run barefooted to the beckoning tree. I shake the branches while Saoirse ducks the shower of apples. Then, using our hands and toes to find the drops in the tall grasses, we quickly gather over two bushels.

I sample one. It is scrumptious. With the taste of success now in my mouth, I abandon all reservations about asking for what I need. We ask everyone we meet if they know where we can find wild apples to harvest. The grandmother of one of Saoirse's friends gets in touch with a downstate resident who owns a second home nearby. The next day, all four of us gather in her front yard and fill my car until we can barely shut the door. Another neighbor directs us to some bordering old pastures, long abandoned, but bursting with fruit. My dad sends us up the road to a spot near where he's been grazing sheep. Our goal for our cider pressing is six bushels of apples. By the end of the second day, the porch at the farm is piled with fourteen bushels. Then Bernie shows up. He's picked enough for himself, and, concerned that our apple dearth would leave us without enough cider for our family, he has picked for us, too. It is our largest apple harvest ever.

The bounty doesn't stop with the apples. Because word of our mission got out, our processing team of three expanded to nine. A second cider press appears on the scene, doubling our production speed, making it easy to ensure that everyone who contributed will have cider for their table. There is plenty of cider for our winter rest, and cider for our neighbors and new friends. Tin cups are passed about as we share in the communion of our bounty, which is extra tasty this year—a perfect balance of sweet and tart, with delightful overtones of generosity and cooperation.

The Endangered Repairman

*I*f there is one piece of electronic equipment in our house that every member of the family equally enjoys, it is our stereo. Listening to music and radio is one of our greatest pleasures. Bob and I purchased it shortly after we got married with gift money we'd received. We chose carefully, selecting a system that had been manufactured in this country, one that we felt would last us for the next fifty years.

It lasted ten. Soon, little buttons stopped working, then a few speaker wires shorted out. This past year, we decided to get it fixed. We contacted the manufacturer.

"Those systems can't be repaired any longer," the company representative informed me. But lucky for Bob and me, the company, keen on seeming "green," has a buy-back program for their old electronic products. They'd take my stereo away, and in exchange, they'd award me a $500 credit toward a new stereo system. I asked if the new ones were still manufactured here. The representative faltered, "Well, no . . ."

We decided to visit a nearby independently owned store that specialized in home entertainment systems. We explained we were looking for a stereo. A good one. There, we learned that stereos were a thing of the past. We were supposed to be listening to music through new wireless blue-tooth speakers that spoke directly to our computers, which would channel the radio stations and music over the Internet. We should just throw out our old stereo and buy the new technology.

"But our Internet is really slow," I started to explain, "and we don't have Internet on the side of the house where we live." The salesman cut me off. He had an answer in the form of an additional electronic device that would magnify the wireless signal and push it into the side of the house where we lived.

"But I don't want to leave my computers and Internet turned on while I'm listening to the radio. And I don't want to have the Internet in that side of my house." Call me kooky, but I don't like to be "connected" at all times. I also don't want to be operating four pieces of electronic equipment (a router, a computer, a signal amplifier and a blue-tooth sound system) just so I can listen to some local folk music over the airwaves.

"What are you lady, Amish? Times are changing!" The salesman snapped at me.

Needless to say, he didn't make the sale.

It was my mom who reminded us that we should call Mr. Kleinberger. For years, he and his wife operated an electronics store on Main Street in Cobleskill. I remember going in there as a girl. He had two or three televisions in stock, maybe three or four radios. New products were not his mainstay. His real bread and butter was in repairing electronics. Any electronics: televisions, radios, VCRs, electric fence chargers. Eventually, the repair business fell away. "Factories don't authorize repair people anymore," Mr. Kleinberger explained to me over the phone. "It used to be that we'd get trained by the manufacturers to repair and maintain their equipment. Nobody does that anymore. They wanna sell you the next new thing . . . I can look at your stereo," he said, "but I can't make any promises."

Bob and I figured we had nothing to lose. We brought it over to his farmhouse, where he directed us to leave it on his kitchen counter, next to a pile of fence chargers, now his bread-and-butter, that local farmers had brought in for resuscitation.

A few weeks later, I called to see how he was progressing. "Nobody at the company will talk to me," he complained. "I called the manufacturer twice to find out how I'm supposed to open the casing on this thing without breaking it, and they tell me they're under strict orders not to release the information. But they'll give you money for it if you wanna buy a new system . . . Seems a waste, though, because if I could open this up, I'm pretty sure the repair would be just a few dollars' worth of parts. A new system would cost you thousands."

Mr. Kleinberger didn't give up. He kept calling the manufacturer, and kept calling, and kept calling. One day a few weeks back, my phone rang. I picked up the receiver, and heard classical music playing. "Ya here that?" Mr. Kleinberger's voice came over the line, "that's your stereo. It's a beautiful piece of machinery, that thing is. Every single part is a standard American part, made here, and easily replaced."

He went on to tell me his story of the repair. He'd made six different phone calls to the manufacturer, each time trying to get the same information: how to open the housing of the stereo without breaking it. Each time, the answer was the same: "We don't service those stereos anymore, and we don't have that information. But we'd be happy to tell you about our buy-back program . . . "

Eventually, Mr. Kleinberger decided that, since he likes to talk, he'd wear them down with his gift of gab. "I told them my whole life story," he said. He talked about his repair shop; about his wife, who has Alzheimer's, who he takes care of; about how he fixes electronics out of his house; about the history of electronics repairs and manufacturing in this country; about his cats. "I figured I'd make 'em crazy," he told me. I could hear his smile, even through the receiver. "And maybe they'd transfer me to someone else. And they did. And I just kept doing it to the next person and the next person. But the first question I'd ask was, 'How long have you worked there?' I finally found one guy, Josh (not his real name), who'd worked there about as long as you had that stereo. That was the longest time of anyone I'd spoken with. I figured I had my man. He remembered when the stereos were manufactured here."

Josh wasn't authorized to release the pertinent information. But like Mr. Kleinberger, he had a love for electronics. This love isn't the narrow obsession with technology that drives so many folks to buy things they don't need. Josh and Mr. Kleinberger shared a mutual passion for the way things are made: the way the right parts make for a quality piece of equipment; the excitement of deciphering a problem and figuring out a repair. Josh held out as long as he could. He reminded Mr. Kleinberger he was under strict orders not to release the information. He told him about the buy-back offer. But with their common love, the information Mr. Kleinberger needed eventually came out. And the stereo was repaired. For 54 bucks.

I've been thinking about Josh and Mr. Kleinberger a lot these days. Every morning, my inbox is filled with urgent messages—online petitions to stop ecologically harmful practices; online petitions to change government policies to benefit the earth; online petitions to save the polar bears. Yet I don't see any online petitions to save people like Josh and Mr. Kleinberger. While I care about the polar bears (and yes, I sign the petitions), Josh and Mr. Kleinberger are an endangered species in their own right, worthy of our attention. The polar bears are in danger because of the way we live, because of our abuses to the environment, because of our throw-away consumer culture. Josh and Mr. Kleinberger are unsung heroes in battling those exact problems. They are the lingering vestiges of our fix-it culture. And we need to bring people like that back into our communities. While "buy-back" programs make a manufacturer appear earth-friendly in the consumer marketplace, they really only stimulate more consumption. A more civic and ecologically sound approach would be to reinstate training programs for independent repair businesses. Locally-owned repair shops help to circulate money throughout the community, help residents lower their cost of living and reduce consumerism and the volume of toxic landfills.

With people like Josh and Mr. Kleinberger around, I think I could get another fifty years out of this stereo . . . maybe even more. Who knows. *Sigh.* It seems they just don't make stereos, or people, like that anymore.

Coping with Envy

$\mathcal{S}$ince the time we published *Radical Homemakers*, a controversial book about ecologically sustainable, values-centered living, Bob and I have frequently felt waves of squeamish guilt. In that tome, I outlined the ways in which the productive, largely self-reliant household can minimize our environmental impact, build community resilience, and rekindle contentment at the home hearth. But now that I have so thoroughly researched the topic and so widely extolled the virtues of radical homemaking in publications, lecture circuits, and interviews, we've felt the pressure to become paragons of this lifestyle. But I wrote the book, in which I interviewed 20 families along the continuum of anti-consumerism, because I believe in the revolutionary power of radical homemaking, *not* because we, ourselves, are experts at living this way.

Rather than typifying the exemplary self-reliant anti-consumerist family, we put our notions of failure and insecurity aside, and focus instead on where we want to go, what we want to do next, inspired by the knowledge of so many others who have succeeded. Looking around our home, there are plenty of signs that we haven't got this lifestyle down to a science. Most of the blueberry bushes limped through the winter, but I lost two of them owing to my imperfect stewardship from prior years (an improved loss rate, if I do say so myself). One of Bob's six beehives died out because he divided the colony at the wrong time last year (Hooray! Only one died this time!). This year's mistakes are already forthcoming: sitting cozy by the fire last February, we decided to plant a small orchard and mail-ordered eleven trees. That was a stupid thing to do. It is fine to decide to plant an orchard, but that decision means the next growing season should be devoted to preparing the soil for the *subsequent* year, not to simply planting and watering baby trees. In our zeal, we skipped an all-important step, and now those poor trees must struggle to survive in soil that is nutrient-poor and nearly devoid of microbial life.

This is not to say we are *complete* failures as radical homemakers. There are some things we're pretty good at. One hive died out, but the others have survived, with no chemical inputs. Later today, I'll be down at the farm making some of the best-tasting sausage to be found in the region. We're great at getting along with our extended family, turning out home-cooked, locally-sourced and healthful meals, sharing resources, educating our kids, and managing our finances to guarantee there is cash for the things that matter. But the truth is, there is *always* someone who does it better.

We had lunch with such a family a few weeks ago, the Luhrmans. They are amazing. Raymond and Sarah met while she was in the Peace Corps in Africa, and set their sights on organic farming. With relatively few resources at their disposal, they found Karl, a farmer interested in seeing his unused land transitioned to a new generation that would farm sustainably. They worked out a flexible and affordable land transfer. By reading books and talking to friends, Raymond figured out how to build a timber-framed Dutch barn. When they realized their finances were not going to allow for the construction of a house, they made the loft into a beautiful, small, energy-efficient family home that can keep them cozy through Northeastern winters on a single cord of firewood. Their electric needs are supplied off-grid by a small windmill and a tiny solar array that they installed themselves. The soil on the land they work is positively alive with microbial activity, their crops are bountiful and nutrient-rich, and their burgeoning CSA has taken off. Their homeschooled daughter Johanna is lovely, their hands skilled and powerful, their souls beautiful.

By the end of our visit, we'd worked out some arrangements to help take care of each other's children as our growing seasons allowed. Smiling warmly, we loaded up our girls and drove away, enthused that such wonderful people were living nearby.

Then it happened, on the drive home. Bob and I both tried to suppress it, but we couldn't stop it. We didn't mean for it to boil up inside us, but there it was: A wicked case of envy.

They must have money from somewhere. They must have some advantage that we didn't have. They must have some wretched, horrible secret we don't know about. There must be something imperfect about these people . . . some reason that they were able to do everything so much better and smarter than we could.

These thoughts were horrible. I liked these people!

I reflected on the phenomenon of envy. What is it, actually? In truth, it is nothing more than admiration with a splash of poison thrown in. But where was the poison coming from?

Ourselves, of course. It came from our own insecurities and imperfections. We didn't try to hand-hew our own house. We didn't feel skilled enough to tackle off-grid technology. If we tried to subsist entirely on *my* gardening efforts, we'd starve.

I wondered what would happen if we could separate the poison of our insecurities from the admiration we felt and which these folks justly deserved. We needed to explore our self-doubts with self-love.

When we did, we saw something totally different. These insecurities were actually tied to our ambitions and dreams—things that Bob and I think are important, things that we would still like to learn. If we had it to do all over again, we'd probably do a lot of things differently. As it is, we don't need to build another house, and going off-grid with our solar array is not the most important move for us to make right now. Those things, however, are tied to deeper aspirations. We want to learn to do more with our hands. We want to tackle challenging self-reliance projects without fear and self-doubt. We want to live harmoniously with our land and become more beneficent creatures to the Earth.

Understanding this, we looked back over our visit. What was waiting for us after we put aside our envy?

Inspiration.

In place of our envy, we discovered a deeper understanding of what's possible, of how wonderful it would be for this planet if more people were able to make better decisions than we have. The envy melted away, and was replaced by a renewed energy for what we can learn, what we can improve today, what we can work toward in the coming growing season, in the coming years.

With a lighter step, I make my way out to the blueberry bushes to test the soil and see how I can nurse them through my past mistakes. Bob cleans out the dead hive and readies for his new colony. He preps the ground for a new top-bar hive, this year's experiment in more humane bee-keeping. We bring manure up from the farm to build up organic matter; we mix compost, dried blood, rock phosphate, and green sand into the soil where we planted the baby trees, and hope for the best. For good measure, we till up a new plot of ground that will be planted with cover crops for the time being, in hopes of maybe doing things right for whatever we plant next year. We put our notions of failure and insecurity aside, and focus instead on where we want to go, what we want to do next, inspired by the fact that there are others who have succeeded, despite their own litany of missteps on their path forward toward a more enjoyable life.

Wednesday Afternoons

As best I can figure, *Madame* and Helmuth moved up here about 15 years ago upon their retirement. They promptly sought out our farm and became regular customers. Soon after that, they assertively opened the door of friendship to us, and we began to learn more about them. Helmuth spoke very little, and *Madame* spoke with deliberation. They were *always* polite. Unlike us, they were also always neat. Their house was impeccably clean. Their clothing was spotless, *Madame's* long white hair always in a neat twist on the back of her head. Such behavior and appearances spurred us to try to curtail our own invectives, to strive to spare them from the bubbling soup of emotion in which our family farm life perpetually simmers. We didn't always succeed. Nevertheless, the friendship continued to grow, and we soon began car-pooling together to appointments, where they'd witness our occasional outbursts of raucous laughter or, to our embarrassment, vituperation. And yet they weren't frightened away. They continued to make a place for us in their well-ordered lives.

From a polite distance, they watched Bob and I become parents, they watched my mom and dad become grandparents. Knowing Bob and I had little money to outfit our layette, and realizing that we were keen on minimizing our ecological impact, they organized families from downstate who were looking to pass along their toys and baby clothes, perused the offerings at their church rummage sales, and filled our dressers and toy closet for years to come, before my first baby was even born. (Saoirse is now nine, and to this day I've still never had to purchase her a single pair of snow pants.) *Madame* and Helmuth continued to buy our meat and eggs, and were first-hand witnesses as I moved from conventional medicine to home birthing, to the holistic care of my family, to my choice to homeschool, to my evolution as a writer with radical ideas.

And when Saoirse was five, *Madame*, a former French teacher, insisted on beginning lessons with my children.

I accepted, but I was resistant to the idea. My own insecurities, along with *Madame's* and Helmuth's formal demeanor, led me to fear they did not approve of our lifestyle choices. I wondered if she saw Bob and me as poor ignoramuses, targets for charity. I wondered if she felt she needed to save Saoirse from our fringe lunatic choice to keep her out of the public school system.

At the same time, I wasn't inclined to pass up an opportunity to enrich my daughter's education. I let my mom drive her the three miles to their house on Wednesday afternoons, where *Madame* and Helmuth dedicated an entire room as a *salle de classe*, where a pot of tea was presented with every lesson.

But I couldn't (or wouldn't) make Saoirse do her homework, and I hadn't taught her to write or read yet, and I grew self-conscious and suspected that *Madame* greatly disapproved of our "un-schooling" educational tactics. I grew defensive about French lessons, perturbed whenever *Madame* would call to ask me questions about my plan of education. When it was my turn to drive Saoirse over, I would often forget. At the same time, in spite of her own lack of linguistic progress, Saoirse eagerly looked forward to her visits. But she never talked about what she learned. "She's very fancy," was the only thing she'd tell me.

Madame and Helmuth stood together picking up their chickens one afternoon when I finally burst into a spate of apologies. "I'm sorry," I said, ready to accept that these lessons were failing. "I can't even get Saoirse to tell me what you *do* in your lessons, let alone help her with any homework." I was ready to quit.

They both nodded in their quiet way. After a moment of awkward silence, *Madame* spoke slowly, softly and carefully. "I care about your children. I care about them very much. I have never had any of my own. And I would like to be able to feel as though they are my own grand-children. I hope you will continue to let me teach them."

And then I understood. *Madame* didn't disapprove of our way of life. She didn't mistrust me as an educator. She simply wanted the freedom to love my children. And so we went forward, my heart lightened by the fact that she and Helmuth only wanted to have a role in Saoirse's and Ula's lives. Wednesday afternoons became one of the most important appointments on our weekly calendar.

As Ula grew into her own readiness to learn French, *Madame* and I evolved to teach together. She worked individually with the girls teaching vocabulary and grammar; I worked in a separate room helping them with conversation. Helmuth would periodically inter-rupt the teaching schedules with requests to teach the girls how to find chanterelles and wild ramps, or with the simple choice to join us for tea and conversation. After lessons, the girls would sit and color, and *Madame* and I would speak in French, both of us eager to keep our skills alive. I grew to love her decorum, and as I confronted my own life dramas—from family deaths and illnesses, to farm stress, to homeschooling travails, I found my soul soothed by her equanimity. In turn, she endured my tattered Carhartts, disheveled hair and per-petually bare feet (but she kept a spare pair of slippers in a drawer where I worked, just in case).

I came to cherish our Wednesday afternoons together.

And while I fully understand that nothing can go on forever, I will admit to my perpetual quiet hopes that it would, that *Madame* and Helmuth would see Saoirse and Ula grow into adulthood.

But the call came early last week that Helmuth had suffered a cerebral hemorrhage, that he was in a coma in the hospital. We drove to the hospital to be with *Madame*, to say our good-byes to Helmuth. The space was cramped, filled with friends and neighbors who'd arrived to lend their love and support. We took turns with *Madame* as she kept her vigil over Helmuth, until family was able to arrive that night.

Saoirse and Ula drew pictures to hang up across from Helmuth's bed. Neighbors brought in comforting music. Members of their church came and read passages from the Bible. All of us wept. And *Madame* received each of us with grace. She held Saoirse and Ula, and they hugged and cried together.

My compulsion in such cases is to fixate on food. Habitual "doers" like myself need activity at such times, and I returned home to my kitchen and channeled my energy into boiling eggs, chopping onions, making broth, searing meat, intent on providing *Madame* with sustenance for her vigil. Helmuth passed away before I could even finish the broth and peel the eggs.

It goes without saying that our Wednesday French lessons were cancelled last week. Instead, Saoirse and Ula joined me in the kitchen. They, too, needed to feel as though there was something they could do. As I put together the stew and deviled eggs for *Madame* and her family, they worked to make a batch of brownies. Determined there should still be color in *Madame's* world, they decorated them with purple frosting and pink, yellow and green sprinkles.

We showed up at *Madame's* house later that Wednesday afternoon, carried our food up to her refrigerator, then came down and sat with her and her family.

Madame's formality melted away. She pulled Saoirse and Ula to her, her arms around one, the other piled into her frail lap.

At the end of our visit, in an impulse to cling to the familiar and grasp for normalcy, I asked *Madame* if she would like me to take some of the French books home, so there would be some continuity in Saoirse and Ula's education while she worked through all that she faced. She packed up a bag of books, gave me a list of assignments to complete, and we went on our way.

I left the books on the floor of my office when we got home. I was determined to try my best, but deeply saddened that I would be tackling the subject alone.

But my mom and dad were visiting with *Madame* yesterday afternoon. And as they left, she gave them a message for me. "Tell Shannon that I will see her and the girls this coming Wednesday afternoon, at three o'clock."

"She needs this now," my mom assured me. "It's important to her to be with the girls, to have structure in her life." I nodded quietly in agreement. What I failed to mention was how much I needed this myself. But I suspect *Madame* was fully aware of this fact.

And so, in spite of our loss of Helmuth, our Wednesday afternoons continue. And with the comfort of conjugations and *vocabulaire*, Saoirse and Ula will be reminded how their choice to learn isn't just about collecting facts. It is an expression of love. And *Madame* and I will find a way to continually strengthen our fragile souls through our surprising friendship.

Culture Clash

Naked Rules

*S*wimming lessons at the village pool start next week. I'm 95 percent confident the girls understand that bathing suits *will* be worn.

They've grown up in a clothing-optional house (grown-ups do tend to stay clothed . . . usually). Naked children are far easier to wash up than stained and dirty clothes, and when given the option, Saoirse and Ula (and their friends) seem to find nudity a far more functional fashion.

But the best part of this household policy is seeing their uninhibited regard for their bodies. They haven't learned to be ashamed of them. It's quite the opposite, in fact. Saoirse, who is nearing the start of puberty, often shares with me that she is looking forward to experiencing the changes in her body. "I think women's bodies are just beautiful," she often effuses. An artist at her core who is smitten with light, contrast and color, she whispers to me, "I love all the soft curves you get to have. I love how your shadow is different from Daddy's."

I'm delighted to see the joy they take in their bodies, and to witness their openness to the growth and change they will experience; but I've done my fair share of sending mixed messages. The clothing Bob and I have made available to my girls is modest. Skirts are long, shirts cover bellies, and nothing skimpier than a tank top has been permitted when we leave the house.

I never thought about the inconsistency until we traveled around the South of France this past spring. At the seashore, Saoirse and Ula enjoyed the same freedom to swim *au naturel* there as at our farm pond back home (which would never happen at a public pool or beach here in the U.S.). Unlike Americans, French parents didn't worry about lugging around giant bags filled with changes of clothing, towels, sunscreen and bathing suits for their children. If they wound up at a beach, many kids just stripped off their clothing and ran into the water (so did a few adults). They ran about until they were dry, and brushed off the sand prior to putting their clothes back on.

At the same time Saoirse and Ula were drinking up their public freedom to be naked, they began noticing the southern French fashions—in particular, off-the-shoulder, short-cropped peasant blouses that left bellies and arms open to the warm air and salty breeze. "They're BEAUTIFUL!" Saoirse gushed to me.

"Don't even think about it," came my priggish reply.

"But aren't bellies just lovely?" she challenged me. "I think it's just gorgeous how the fabric looks next to the bare skin on bellies."

Here's the conflict I have as a mom: I want my daughters to love and respect their bodies, to feel as comfortable with their clothing off as they do with it on. I'm all for naked swimming, I don't mind when they play dress up with tutus and nothing else, and I smile at their nude bodies as they dance around the woods behind our house. But there are expectations in this country that our children (as well as grownups) will remain covered at all times when in public. As a culture, we are fearful of our nakedness. In addition to that, I am wary of skimpy fashions, of how people with less-than-honorable intentions might leer at my beautiful little girls. I am anxious that my daughters might dress in a way that makes them look older than they actually are, that their choice to wear skimpier clothes (or to leave essential articles out all together) might invite some kind of trouble.

And daily, my daughters challenge that paranoia. Ula thinks underpants are a senseless joke, and often forgets to wear them under her skirts. She regards clothing as having little more than costume value ("What's the point of undies? Nobody even sees them!"). Saoirse sees her body as another venue to express her creativity and her zest for life. While she occasionally expresses some new-found modesty, she is just as likely to think it perfectly acceptable to head with me to the bank wearing underpants and her beloved diaphanous glitter scarf as a toga. These girls haven't encountered the uglier side of the world, and I am finding myself, particularly in the warm summer months, constantly trying to negotiate the natural acceptance of naked bodies, my own apprehensions, and the cultural expectations outside our home.

I don't have it down. I've had talks with Saoirse in which I've tried to explain some of my concerns about confusing people by looking older than she actually is (which is a very hard conversation to have without frightening a child). I've grown more frank about pointing out when some of her homemade wardrobe pieces "malfunction" too severely for public use. We've agreed that she and her sister are permitted to dress (or not dress) as they like at home, but that I get final say over all wardrobe choices leaving the house. That doesn't mean we haven't had a few screaming matches in the driveway over my decisions. It is happening more often as Saoirse grows more independent. There are rules to the unspoken dress code that I haven't yet successfully articulated. I keep trying, but there are many corollaries and addenda to each rule that we grown-ups tacitly understand, but that kids see as patent inconsistencies. However, they do understand that when we head to the village pool for swimming lessons next week, we change in the girls' locker room, *not* by the car, *not* at a picnic bench, and suits remain on at all times poolside.

This should be an improvement over prior years (er . . . I suspect we garnered a bit of a reputation down there last season). But as for the crop-top peasant blouses, I did eventually give in. Once I saw the fashions through Saoirse's eyes, I couldn't help but agree. Those girls have some beautiful little bellies—why not let them enjoy them?

Acting Out

$\mathcal{S}$aoirse and Ula are three years apart. Saoirse, nearly nine, is unusually tall, slender, well-spoken, and comes across to grown-ups as particularly well-behaved and extraordinarily poised. Ula isn't any of those things. At 5, she's about a foot shorter than her sister, demonstrates an ability to move exceptionally heavy objects for a child of her proportions, has a wandering eye that appears to have a mind of its own, wears glasses, and acts strictly on impulse. I have been mulling over how I am supposed to help her work with that last attribute.

A few days ago, Ula and her best friend Katharine were having a tea party in the living room. Saoirse, who can't help but be admired, adored and obeyed by all younger children (except, of course, her sister), interrupted the tea party with a sing-song announcement: "It's puzzle hour, kids! Now we're all going to put puzzles together!" She proceeded to open up a series of jigsaw puzzles and push aside the tea party. Ula didn't warm to the idea. She began pitching cardboard puzzle pieces at her sister. Katharine joined her.

Saoirse stormed off in frustration, seeking adult intervention. Bob and I didn't yell at anyone. We just helped Saoirse find a quiet space where she could have some alone time free from non-compliant five-year-olds. Later on, after Katharine went home and we were sitting quietly together with Ula, Bob opened the conversation, suggesting that throwing puzzle pieces at her sister wasn't an appropriate response to the situation, no matter how bossy her sister was being. He looked to me for back-up commentary. I avoided his eyes and tried not to laugh. "That's right, Daddy," I tried to muster. I casually covered my mouth so Ula wouldn't see it twitch. But Daddy saw it. And he couldn't control it either. We both burst into laughter. Ula patiently waited for her scolding to resume. We tried a second time with a few weak platitudes, like "throwing things is never appropriate." Trouble was, Bob and I both agreed that it would be very hard for either of us to resist hurling puzzle pieces in a similar situation . . . "puzzle time" over a tea party? She'd had it coming to her! And Ula knew it. "Look," Bob finally said. "We're not really angry with you; but you need to find different ways to express your frustration, OK?" Ula agreed.

Yesterday, Ula and her friend Katharine were again playing, this time with a kitchen set out on the porch at the farm. They had a bowl of water and rocks for soup stock. Saoirse entered the scene to join the fun, and proceeded to direct the girls as to what they could and could not do with that water. Ignoring her, Ula picked up a spoon and sipped her broth, then picked up the bowl and quaffed a more satisfying drink. Saoirse proceeded to reprimand her. Ula quietly obliged and put the spoon down. She disappeared for a few moments. Saoirse and Katharine thought nothing of it and resumed play. Without a word, Ula returned to the porch a few minutes later and rejoined the game. But three hours later, Saoirse pushed her digital camera in front of my face. "Look!" She exclaimed.

Apparently, Ula had taken to heart Bob's suggestion that she find a different way to express her frustration. This time, she drew upon her more creative sensibilities. She'd taken her sister's camera, deleted some of the images, then used the freed-up electrons to photograph her naked hiney, the captured image a close up of her own vertical smile. Saoirse was half-heartedly trying to rat out her sister, but mostly, all she could do was laugh and recount exactly how she'd managed to incite the crime.

As a homeschooling mom, I occasionally envy non-homeschooling parents who have the luxury of blaming outside influences for their children's shortcomings. Bad behavior or academic failure can conveniently be blamed on the school bus, other schoolchildren, negligent teachers, misspent school resources, misguided school boards, pinched school budgets. Bob and I have none of those excuses. If our children don't learn successfully or behave badly, the blame falls squarely on our shoulders.

Thus, Ula's behavior falls back to Bob and me. And I am of two minds about how to address it. I suppose I should play the part of "good mom" and have a serious talk with her about appropriate and inappropriate ways of dealing with frustration. Perhaps I should explain just what I learned in school: *it is not appropriate to act out.*

But I can't quite bring myself to do this. Deep down, I feel one of the biggest problems with our culture is that we *don't* act out. We've been so conditioned to "behave appropriately" that many of us have lost the instinct to identify and point out absurdity when it transpires before our eyes. As an example, I delivered a keynote presentation at an organic farming conference this past winter. Before I took the podium, the state secretary of agriculture gave the opening address. In it, he stood before an auditorium packed with organic farmers and told them that if they wanted to have success with their conference that day, and with their businesses in the future, then the first thing they needed to learn was that they should *never* speak ill of or publicly criticize the conventional food system.

Here was absurdity. A perfect justification for acting out. But not one person did. Instead, when he finished, he was given a tepid round of polite applause. I regret that I didn't have the gumption to take the podium and directly call attention to the balderdash we had just been fed. I was too polite. After all, *I was raised not to act out.* My skills at calling attention to absurdity are above average, but nowhere near as honed as I'd like them to be.

Ula demonstrates what developmental specialists would probably identify as the typical impulse control issues of a five-year-old. I can't help but consider it a gift. Maybe throwing cardboard puzzle pieces or mooning a camera are considered inappropriate responses in an adult world. But I think they were relatively reasonable choices for a five-year-old. Ula is learning to identify absurdity. Saoirse is learning to negotiate the limits of her power as a result. As the parent, I choose to step back and let them play it out, and I accept full accountability for this choice.

Alpha Female

*D*usky was *not* supposed to be our dog. It was Grammie, who, for years, has wanted a little lap dog. But the girls and I were the ones who went to pick up the miniature mutt. And despite my bias against tiny dogs, this fuzzy black smudge, part Yorkshire terrier and part poodle, made a strong impression in the cute department.

The girls should *not* have made that drive with me. I should *not* have allowed them to play with her on the ride home. I should *not* have allowed them to cuddle and bond with the puppy that first hour until Grammie was able to finally come greet her new companion.

And most of all, Grammie should *not* have taken pity on Saoirse's wide eyes as they grew teary around the corners when the puppy was lifted from her arms. Grammie should *not* have paid attention to Ula's dramatic wails of despair as she sat down on the porch to nuzzle the little dream dog that her heart had longed for these past 25 years.

Because that's what led to Dusky coming home to *our* house instead. Grammie couldn't bear to remove the puppy from her grandchildren, and so, in spite of the fact that we already have the world's most perfect dog (a true mutt of an authentic size), our household this past week has expanded to include Saoirse and Ula's new baby.

And that, of course, explains how it came to be that I now have another morning office companion curled up in my lap as I write this.

This has been an emotional week for me. Spriggan, our long-time family dog, has been my steadfast companion from the day Bob and I brought her home. She has slept beside my desk through every book I've written, walked beside me on the dirt road each and every morning, even sat beside me through the birth of both of my daughters. I am racked with guilt as Dusky commands my attention in order to ensure her proper nourishment, house breaking, and periodic shelter from the girls' affectionate mauling. By giving this new puppy such attendance, I feel as though I am abandoning my best friend.

A visitor to our home this week noted my conflict as I interrupted our conversation when my anti-piddle radar detected that Dusky was seeking out a shady cool spot on the floor to squat. I apologized before leaping from my chair to catch the culprit before the crime was committed, then called Saoirse to take her to the yard. Upon returning, Dusky didn't run off with Saoirse. Rather, she stayed where I was.

"This is *not* my dog," I insisted. "But if I don't want my house littered with dog excrement, I'm finding I need to take control. And suddenly, it feels like I have a new personal pet."

"But of course," observed my guest. "You're the alpha female."

Alpha female. I hadn't considered that. But the idea has stayed at the fore of my mind all this past week as I interrupt my pre-dawn writing sessions with myriad puppy walks, as Dusky has adopted the spot beneath my desk as her hideout, as her kennel has taken up residence on the floor next to my side of the bed, as her head cocks and responds to the sound of my voice, as she promptly responds to even my softest disciplinary utterances of "no" when she attempts to chew the carpet or unwind my knitting. I'm not pushing out my beloved Spriggan. Nor am I usurping my daughters' new pet (because, in truth, they are doing a great job during the day of seeing to Dusky's needs). But in order to maintain a certain amount of order in our family chaos, I simply need to exert some control. It's just my job.

"Alpha female . . . Does this make me a dominant bitch?" I asked Bob over our morning coffee yesterday.

"Oh, no dear," came his prompt reply. "It just *identifies* you as the dominant bitch."

Luckily, I find his barbed humor quite sexy. But many a truth is said in jest. And I'm certain my loving husband isn't the only one who has made such observations about me. But as I look back over this past week in our family's adjustment to Dusky, I see where this behavioral tendency is key to our survival, not just with a new puppy, but in all the messiness that is part of managing a home as a dynamic ecosystem.

Bob's and my choice to center our lives around our home—to keep our children here for their education and balance that against our diversified income strategies; to produce and preserve so much of our own food; to partner with my parents and the land for our livelihood; *and* to remain part of a broader community and family network—can be a logistical nightmare. It takes a certain amount of alpha-behavior to make sure that things happen when they should; that the daily amorphia of tumbling children, piddling puppies, snarling senior pets, hungry farm customers, weedy blueberries, unpainted siding, busy bees, unscheduled playdates, bushels of cucumbers and stalks of dill . . .—eventually take shape into educated kids with resonant relationships, well-mannered dogs, a house that holds up to the sun and snow, enough cash to pay the taxes, and a few jars of pickles for the winter.

I have wondered this week if my lifestyle choices and decision to become a gainfully unemployed, radical homemaking, third-generation farmer-parent pushed me into the role of alpha female, or if my natural tendency toward being an alpha female drove me to eschew a more conventional path in favor of lending my strong spirit toward shaping creative entropy into a more interesting life. I suppose it doesn't really matter which is the case. Playing the part of Alpha Female is how I have managed to survive in my world. It may not always be necessary. Indeed, I look forward to a time when I can surrender the role. But it probably won't happen before this puppy is house-broken. And in the meantime, it helps me to make sure that the needs of my family are met, and that everyone—kids, husband, grandparents, friends, puppies, dogs, cats, and livestock included—are getting the love and attention they deserve.

Crunchy Moms and Health Care

Yesterday afternoon I received a phone call. My daughters are enrolled in a state-subsidized health insurance program, and our family was selected to participate in a national survey about our experience.

My responses to the first few questions would probably have given the surveyors justification to conclude that the program was effective. I reported that my children were in excellent physical and mental health, that they were showing no signs of learning disabilities or emotional disorders. They were not taking any prescription drugs, and they did not have any physical limitations that prevented them from participating in normal childhood activities.

The trouble arose when the interviewer asked me the following (paraphrased—I can't remember the exact wording) question: "How often are the health care providers for your children willing to accommodate for your cultural differences: always, almost always, often, sometimes, almost never, or never?"

I was silent.

"Ms. Hayes? The question was 'How often are the health care providers—'"

"I heard the question," I interrupted. But tears had started to come to my eyes as I thought back over my experiences. "The answer is 'never.'"

Naturally, that led to a series of questions about my race, religion, and education levels. I'm an educated white female. That doesn't fit the profile of someone who might feel culturally marginalized in our health care system. But I'm certain I'm not alone.

My experience began with my first pregnancy, my first extended involvement as an adult in the health care system. I would attend one check-up and be told that everything seemed normal. At a subsequent check-up, I had gained too much weight. At the next check-up, I hadn't gained enough, and I was accused of "starving my baby." I was encouraged to go have a burger and fries at McDonald's. When I asked questions, I was told that I was thinking too much.

The health of my pregnancy was being judged by a parabolic curve, where my various scores—blood pressure, weight, and myriad other numbers—were supposed to fit within two degrees of standard deviation from a narrowly defined norm. The gauge of the tests was whether my scores were normal for a woman of my age—not whether I was healthy. In my seventh month of pregnancy, I began to feel like the system was not conducive to allowing for the natural childbirth I wanted. I read and researched about alternatives to hospital birthing, and concluded that the safest choice for me was to hire a homebirth midwife.

After 24 hours of labor and an extended period of pushing, I was exhausted, and my midwife brought me into the hospital for an IV. Before we were out of the triage room, I gave birth naturally to a healthy baby girl.

Bob and I were packing our belongings to go home the next morning, when suddenly we were surrounded by a pediatrician and two nurses.

"You're not going home," I was informed. "Your daughter has a very serious blood infection. She may have spinal meningitis, and she could die. You most likely contaminated her by birthing at home. You'll be here for 10 days."

For the time being, I'm going to leave the guilt, shock, and despair that I experienced as a brand new mother out of this discussion. We won't talk about the impact it had on my own health. After all, the topic of the survey was my *children's* health. In this particular story, newborn Saoirse was then given a spinal tap. She was put on a drip IV that made it impossible for me to nurse her, and put on a regimen of four different antibiotics. We were under constant surveillance.

At first, I was too shocked to hear the comments from each nurse that came in. But late in the night, a day or two later, one nurse began looking back and forth at her records, double-checking something. "Is there something wrong?" I asked her.

"It's just that, well," the nurse faltered for a moment. "This baby looks very healthy to me. I wanted to make sure this is the right baby. She doesn't have any symptoms." In the dark of night, I began hearing the comments from each nurse that had come through earlier. My baby was beautiful, they'd each said. She didn't look sick. She didn't act sick. The next morning I confronted the nurse on duty.

"I don't think I agree with the diagnosis," I told her. "Can you please tell me my rights?"

"There isn't anything you can do," I was told. "The hospital can take custody of your baby."

There never was a blood infection. The initial sample drawn had been contaminated in the hospital. But what did I learn? That by researching and taking the action that I felt was most conducive to my child's and my health, and choosing to birth at home until a trained midwife felt it was medically necessary to seek hospital assistance, I was regarded by the conventional medical system as a danger to my child.

That was just the start of a long line of experiences that have taught me the following: An educated parent who sees themselves as the primary care practitioner for their children, and therefore takes the time to give care at home first, and opts to read and research before "consuming" services of the health care industry, is not safe in the conventional health care system. My experience has been repeated every time I've had to bring my daughters in for care—an emergency room visit for Saoirse when she was 7 for a farm injury where I agreed to a tetanus vaccine, and the physician ordered a combination tetanus, diptheria and pertussis vaccination without—in fact, contrary to—my consent; a trip to an opthalmologist when I noticed Ula was developing a wandering eye, where I was told to return a few months later to begin exploring surgery (the vastly cheaper and more successful option of vision therapy was not on the table for discussion); the trip to the dentist for Saoirse, where the dentist never spoke to Bob, but simply left word with the receptionist that she was to schedule a return appointment for the unexpected onset of multiple cavities, with no discussion of possible nutrition issues, food allergies, or alternatives to drilling baby teeth.

In each case, Bob and I have been guarded, or even fearful. If we disagree, if we assert our intelligence and our rights, will we be reported for something? Will we be subjected to an investigation? Will temporary custody be taken of our children? To someone more familiar with the system, these may seem like irrational fears. But we confronted this threat once before. Maybe we would have been successful in a dispute, but that is not a chance we wish to take.

We are not alone in our fears. We've met many parents along our radical homemaking path who believe it is their responsibility to be truly informed about all health issues the children in their care may face, who not only question the conventional health care system that has transmogrified into a medical industry, but have come to fear it.

I do not completely reject conventional western medicine. But I do not have blind faith in it, either. When medical issues confront my family, I want to read and research. I will not limit my investigation to positivist science, nor to conventional modern practices. I will have explored the spiritual, emotional, nutritional and environmental issues behind whatever we are confronting. And that makes me (and many folks like me) feel like a cultural anomaly during those times when I must enter into a conventional health care system. That's too bad, because folks like me who read and research widely and who have the most intimate knowledge of their children's health probably have a lot of good information we could bring to the table to improve care in this country . . . if we felt safe enough to share it. But instead, it is fears like mine that may prevent those of us who are part of the self-educating counter-culture from accessing care when it is most needed. In my case, when I can afford it, I take my children to caregivers outside the insurance network who are willing to work with my cultural values and who take my research seriously. But that's a pricey option. Not everyone can afford to make that choice. Thus, even with health insurance, not everyone will get the care they actually need.

And that's the bit of information the survey simply didn't ask about.

Which God Do I Choose?

*I*f asked, I'd have to say that my spiritual education began somewhere down by the creek bed on the farm, where as a child I pondered the flow of water as I filled my palms to drink, or the miracle of the wild raspberries that hung over my rocky perch. But my formal religious education began in second grade, when I was enrolled in a Catholic Sunday school for weekly lessons that would continue through my junior year of high school. At first I enjoyed going. We read stories from the Bible, talked about what they meant, and discussed how they might apply to our daily lives. We learned about different ways to pray, and I developed relationships with a number of community members from my church. But troublesome questions arose when I was 14, and my teacher for that year was particularly zealous in his faith. For the first time, I began to hear repeated references to "sinners," "evil," "the devil." Indeed, this teacher seemed so obsessed with identifying the work of the devil, in hindsight I wonder if he placed more faith in Satan than God. He preached to us about the End Times, which he felt would take place in March of that very year, and exulted about how he relished "the Coming," because sinners would finally be sorted out from "true Christians."

I spent the better part of that academic year in a state of dread and panic. Not least among my many concerns about this end-of-the-world business was the fact that I had been saving for over a year to buy myself a new bicycle. I was shattered to consider that the world would be over before I could take my first spring ride. (I know . . . that seems selfish and materialistic, but hey—I was only a kid.)

My family was outraged when, in a state of total distress, I began recounting the substance of my Sunday school lessons. My grandmother was particularly concerned. I sat at her kitchen counter one afternoon, and she gave me her own version of religious education. "Shannon, if you learn one thing from me, it's this: More people have been killed in the name of God than for any other reason." That's when she introduced me to the other side of my family's religion. We talked about the Crusades, the Inquisition, witch trials. She recited James Henry Leigh Hunt's poem, *Abou Ben Adhem*, then told me that the divine didn't care which religion I chose. Rather, what mattered was how I cared for and loved humankind and the world.

Our conversation never called into question the existence of the divine. Rather, it examined humanity's history of justifying violence, manipulation and coercion by presuming that "God was on their side." I became wary of humans' proclivity for invoking the divine as a justification for exclusion, intolerance, or persecution. But interestingly, my faith grew and expanded as a result. I became more aware of the role my own conscience played in the evolution of my faith.

As an adult, I began to consider that the monotheistic concept of a patriarch god was merely the most fashionable rendition of the form that the divine embodies. We have no proof that spirits of Native American beliefs don't exist, that Greek, Roman and Egyptian gods don't exist, that Hindu gods don't exist, that there is no such thing as a Pagan Goddess, or that fairies don't exist.

I bring this up today, because sitting on my desk is one of many letters I have received over the course of my writing career asking, since my message seems to align with many Christian teachings, that I infuse my work more pointedly with the Word of (the Christian) God.

For several years, I've stayed quiet as these little notes have arrived in my mailbox, been passed to me at conferences following lectures, popped up in my email folder, or appeared publicly in written criticisms of my work. I feel like such propositions are asking me to take sides and favor Christianity over all other faiths. To be honest, I can't help but wonder if those who feel compelled to push me to make such a decision are those least secure with their faith. I have many Christian readers who nourish my mind and spirit daily with their thoughtful responses, and I know they are comfortable enough with their path that they need not ask me to help generate more converts for their religion.

In truth, it warms my heart to know that the ideas I'm promoting—of living in harmony with our earth and our neighbors, about the power of community, about the importance of the hearth—resonate with Christian teachings. And while I embrace Christianity, I do not embrace *only* Christianity. If I advocate any particular faith in my work, then I must wrestle with the idea that I am excluding all the other belief systems that can enrich these ideas. Of course, it is not only Christians who are participating in this discussion. Radical homemakers are Buddhists, Taoists, Muslims, Hindus, Pagans, atheists and agnostics . . . the list goes on. I am deeply thankful that all of them feel the concepts resonate with their beliefs. When, across faiths, we are able to agree to love and honor the earth and our fellow humans, then everyone gains.

As I move forward with my explorations into how we can build a resilient future, about how we can have a meaningful and enjoyable life in the face of climate change and social, political and economic upheaval, I increasingly believe that we will all fare better if we can find a way to allow the divine to infuse our lives. But if we worry about whether other human beings adhere to the same religious doctrine as our own, or whether they name the divine using the same words, we will quickly find ourselves back in the Dark Ages, having failed to learn the lessons that history books (and my grandmother) have taught us about the peril of insisting that we all worship the same God. I'd prefer not to go down that route. If I am a failed Christian by my refusal to be *only* Christian, well, in the spirit of *Abou Ben Adhem*, "I pray thee, then, write me as one that loves [her] fellow men [and women]."

Abou Ben Adhem

Abou Ben Adhem (may his tribe increase!)
Awoke one night from a deep dream of peace,
And saw, within the moonlight in his room,
Making it rich, and like a lily in bloom,
An angel writing in a book of gold:—
Exceeding peace had made Ben Adhem bold,
And to the Presence in the room he said
"What writest thou?"—The vision raised its head,
And with a look made of all sweet accord,
Answered "The names of those who love the Lord."
"And is mine one?" said Abou. "Nay, not so,"
Replied the angel. Abou spoke more low,
But cheerly still, and said "I pray thee, then,
Write me as one that loves his fellow men."
The angel wrote, and vanished. The next night
It came again with a great wakening light,
And showed the names whom love of God had blessed,
And lo! Ben Adhem's name led all the rest.
        – *James Henry Leigh Hunt*

The Good Life

Homespun Mom Comes Unraveled

I wrote this piece in 2007, when my youngest was only 5 months old. Compared to now, we were still relatively new to our radical homemaking lifestyle. I have chosen to re-print it here, because I think it is a good essay for reminding folks how this path can feel at the outset. I'm also rather sentimental about this essay, because it prompted me to go on a quest to research and write the book that became Radical Homemakers.

I completed grad school in 2001 knowing only that I was not cut out for a professional life. The "Supermom" ideal of blending family and career seemed impossible to attain. Instead, Bob and I rejoined my family on our grassfed livestock farm, planted perennial beds and an organic garden, and began pursuing an authentic life— one where we lived by our principles. We split our own firewood; rendered our animal fats to make soap; canned peaches, cider, plums and jellies; stored winter vegetables. He wove baskets. I wrote a cookbook. We started a family, worked on the farm, and sold meat at our weekly farmers' market.

In pursuit of our self-sufficiency, I didn't realize that I had actually become a *type*. Even if we've never met, *you know me*. I am part of a new cadre of women—the Über-Moms. We are the over-educated over-achievers, sidestepping the conventional rat race in favor of an alternative maelstrom. In school we were taught that our careers could be our lives, and instead, we've opted to make our lives our careers. You can see us every week at your farmers' market. When consumers cried out for "food with a face," we stepped forward and offered you our sun-kissed complexions, breast-fed babies and homegrown products. We nourish our families on grassfed meats, homemade kefir, raw farmers' cheese and yogurt; we knit sweaters, sew quilts and hand-stitch Halloween costumes; we gather eggs, milk the family cow, weed the vegetable patch and eviscerate chickens with our babies strapped to our backs; we compost everything from dinner scraps to organic diapers to placentas. Our children are home-birthed, home-fed, and home-schooled. We forbid white flour, white sugar, television, Disney films and plastic toys. We bake wholesome cookies and make believe they taste delicious. We sit on panels at farmer-chef dinners, host workshops and write newsletter articles. We claim to know nothing about cell phones, iPhones or tablets, but we have websites and PowerPoint presentations featuring idyllic pictures of our children bottle feeding lambs or nuzzling chicks. *We blog.*

And when you approach us at the weekly market, we offer to sell you our eggs, homegrown tomatoes, a grassfed steak or a freshly processed chicken. But really, we are selling you more than that. We are selling you our lifestyle. "Buy from me," it feels as though we're saying, "because I represent your values."

But what I really feel like saying is, *"Buy from me, because I want to pick up a bottle of vodka on the way home."* Somehow, on our paths toward this noble life, one more group of girls has fallen prey to another impossible feminine ideal. And I, for one, am crumbling under the pressure of Über-Momming. Our gardens are a mess, my kids are throwing up on the way to the market, my fingers ache from milking the cow, we're running out of homemade soap, and attachment parenting is causing my back to ache. The cat has made a bed in my unfinished knitting, the firewood pile's getting rained on, and despite our best efforts, our four-year-old still longs to be a Disney Princess.

And, truth be told, I don't always feel like passing a summer afternoon making lacto-fermented pickles, stuffing sausages or packing meat for the farmers' market. I want to take my girls swimming in the pond, then sprawl out with them across my bed for a midsummer nap beneath an open window. I want to sip a martini and dance on the screen porch with my husband. I want to put on lipstick, go see a movie with the family, then eat ice cream while watching lightning bugs.

Farming keeps us in a state of sated poverty. We eat well, but cannot afford (and prefer not to afford) conveniences or hire assistance of any kind. *Hired help* violates the Über-Mom code. Instead, our family has settled for a life of radical domestic imperfection. We've quit mowing our lawn. It wastes gas, anyhow. Laundry doesn't really need to be folded. It's easier for my girls to find their clothes when they're strewn across the couch. We'll still eat grassfed meat, but we can't worry about cleaning up the drippings that stick to the bottom of the refrigerator. And maybe if we ignore those organic vegetables rotting in the produce drawer, they'll manage to compost themselves. I just don't invite any Über-Moms over for lunch.

So next time when you see me at the farmers' market, please don't marvel wide-eyed at my seemingly pristine, wholesome, puritanical lifestyle. Smile and thank me for the succulent pork chops, beautifully marbled steaks or the tasty eggs, then put your hand on my arm, lean forward and remind me that you are not buying from me because I am an ideal archetype representing your values. You are buying from me because I am your friend, your neighbor, a responsible producer, and the girl you can turn to for a nice juicy piece of meat. And a perfect martini.

The Smell of Mud Season

It's mud season . . . that time of year when those of us who have been slumbering right along with Mother Earth roll over and discover that she, too, suffers from a wicked case of morning breath.

The manure in the barnyard, so dependably solid throughout the ice and snow of winter, grips our feet as we carry hay to the livestock, releasing pungent odors of pigs, sheep and cows. We greet each other with shrieks at the kitchen door. "Take off your boots! You're tracking manure, and you *stink!*"

Mother Earth's morning breath is not limited to the barnyard. The woodpile, too, suddenly damp, gives off a musty odor, along with the moldering leaves and newly stirring bug colonies residing in the crevasses. The compost pile, mounded high with the carcasses of all our winter feasts and in desperate need of turning, releases her own unique aroma of grit and rot as she simmers away in the morning sun.

Like a newly wakened bedfellow, I take in these mud season scents and feel inclined to block them—to roll over with my pillow over my head and wish for my winter's rest to continue.

But Mother Earth, herself seemingly weary of being stagnant too long, will not cooperate. As the snow and ice trickle away from the edges of the fields and forests, the smell of the soil itself gently emanates up from the ground. Hardly discernible at first, this odor is not foul, but sweet. The scent of heat and moisture seeping through the fertile ground is so unmistakable and irresistible, no matter how fiercely my body longs to rest, I cannot resist the opportunity to draw in my breath. I stop wherever I detect it and inhale. Like a fresh pot of coffee, this smell of the earth is more persuasive than the warmth of down blankets and pillows, more enticing than winter's slumber. It beckons—*it is time to come out and grow.*

The Good Life Can Be a Messy Life

I woke up this morning and came down to my office in the pre-dawn darkness. I should have done yoga. I should have meditated. Instead, I fixed my attention on the wood stove. It's late May, for Pete's sake, I shouldn't need a fire. But I couldn't stop shivering. I stumbled through the dark outside until I had some kindling and firewood. Without even realizing I was doing it, I came back inside, and fabricated an excuse to wake up Bob and ask for his help.

He came downstairs bleary-eyed and dutiful, tripping over the dog bones and scraps of kid projects littering the floor. I groped my way through the curtain of laundry that was hung to dry from the tie rods on the ceiling and met him halfway. And there I fell into his arms, clung to his waist, and burst into tears.

"I had a bad dream," I whimpered. "You left me."

"Where'd I go?"

"Back to grad school."

"I think that would be *my* idea of a bad dream. You forget how bad grad school was for me."

"No," I giggled, still crying, "you got tired of all this. All the mess and all the chaos, and all the busyness. So you just slipped away, rented a room someplace, and that was that. And I was so busy, you were gone a month before I realized it."

"I'm not going anywhere."

And then he held me and I cried and cried and cried some more. Some days, I need the cry more than the yoga.

It's spring. In the past six weeks, the longest stretch of time I've had alone with my husband has been the 45-minute drive to our farmers' market, which opened this past weekend. He's gone every morning to help at the farm, while I remain behind to see to homeschool lessons, weeding, yard work, planting, kids' activities, bookkeeping, appointments, errands, customer correspondence, and fixing lunches, in between work sessions to make sausage, pâté, soap, salve and candles for the market.

The grass has grown half-way up my shins, the kitchen cabinets seem permanently sticky from slap-dash efforts to clean up from last week's honey bottling disaster, the dishes are piling up, soap batter has spilled and hardened to my kitchen counters, I'm riddled with guilt over explaining to Ula that she is NOT helping me out by dumping all of her plush toys in the center of the living room so that she can help me relax by performing a puppet show, and I'm beginning to wonder if Saoirse will ever understand long division before she turns 21. Oh, and my oldest dog is now incontinent, needs medication twice a day, refuses to take it, and confronts me at the beginning and end of each day with a locked jaw that requires a level of mutual coercion and bullying that she and I have never encountered in our 13-year friendship.

As I write all this, I think back to my life with Ruth and Sanford, elderly subsistence farmers who lived up the road from us and took me on as a granddaughter-of-choice when I was a youngster. Any time that I wasn't in school I could be found up in their pastures, out in their barn, mowing their grass, or sitting at their kitchen table.

Ruth and Sanford were very influential in this life I've chosen. I remember vividly realizing how all the pressures I faced with school life would fall away from me as I walked the mile up the road to their farm on Saturdays and Sundays. When there, time seemed to stand still, I was able to breathe, be a part of my ecosystem, and feel entirely free. Nothing ever felt hurried. My worries vanished.

But here I am, trying to model my life after their path, and I feel breathless as I try to make my way through each day. What's different?

They were subsistence farmers living on just a few thousand dollars per year. We're small-scale production farmers. When I knew them, there were no longer children living in their home. And when kids did live on the farm, they left on a school bus every day. I've chosen to homeschool mine, and have accepted the time commitment that entails. I've also chosen to accept the creative challenge of being a writer. But the biggest difference, I suspect, has to do with the fact that every spring, while Ruth and Sanford confronted the majority of the repairs, the tilling, the chores, the planting and the calving, I was tucked away at school, completely oblivious to what they faced. My only exposure was on the weekends and summers. By virtue of being a child, I was spared the difficulties that all grown-ups encounter with this way of life.

Contrary to my memory, time never stood still for Ruth and Sanford. It only stood still for me, because their life represented a "vacation" of sorts from my school world. And as a result, I developed an image in my mind of what this life was supposed to be: ample time on the back porch, a rocking chair with a pile of knitting, naturally well-behaved children who clean up after themselves and dutifully study their lessons without my intervention, old dogs who sigh contentedly and don't pee on the rug, well-crafted books and essays that seem to write themselves, gardens that weed themselves, a husband who is never too busy or too tired to light a tiny fire for his wife in the wee hours of a chilly May morning.

Even if these romantic ideals can't be realized on a daily basis, they are still important. They are my reminders of what I desire, of why I chose this path. Even if I'm crying in my husband's arms in the chilly dark hours of an early morning, I know this is still what we want. He wants to be outside fixing and tinkering. I want to pull the weeds. He wants to tend the bees. I want to write and teach my kids. He wants to weave baskets and stack fire-wood. I want to plant a garden and cook. We want to drive to our farmers' market every Saturday, we want to see our family thrive, we want to live on this place, within this place and be of this place.

So when the sticky cabinets are finally wiped down, the garden is finally planted, the chores are done, the day's essay is written and the sun has warmed the earth enough to allow Bob and me a brief moment to sit quietly on the porch, the respite we've earned will feel all that much sweeter, because we will have come by it honestly, tiring ourselves by doing the things we have chosen.

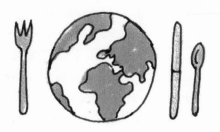

Feeding the World

*S*ooner or later the question comes up. Whether it is between two friends sharing a stew made from local grassfed beef and their garden harvest, customers and vendors at a farmers' market, livestock farmers gathered on a pasture walk, neighbors working together to tend a flock of backyard chickens, or organic vegetable producers discussing yields at a conference, someone will eventually ask, "But can we feed the world this way?"

As those of us in the sustainable agriculture movement try to draw humanity away from thoughtless extraction of the earth's resources, and toward a way of life that honors the earth and all of her creatures, I think this is the most maddening question we can be asking ourselves. Nevertheless, we've all been conditioned to reflexively pose this question as if to gauge the validity of our methods as we seek to cleave new paths toward sustainability.

However, 75 or 100 years ago, such a question would never have entered into our dialogue. To ask a local farmer or homesteader how his or her production methods could feed the world would have been an absurdity. The local producer's job was to support the family, the community, and his or her bioregion, *not* the world.

But following World War II, with the onset of the "Green Revolution," feeding the world became a national mantra. It was a ubiquitous "good" that handily justified discovery that the petro-chemicals developed in wartime could find post-war applications if dumped on our food supply. "Feeding the world" consoled farmers as they incurred mountains of debt to afford the fossil fuel-intensive machinery and expansive acreage that would enable them to crank out tons of food, for which they would garner increasingly lower prices. "Feeding the world" was the elixir offered as our grandparents attempted to adjust their palates to a food supply that was suddenly tasteless as commodity product replaced local food in the market. "Feeding the world" was the slogan tossed about as rural people the world over surrendered ties to the land, moved to cities, and trusted that the food system would take care of itself. "Feeding the world" was the background tune playing in the bank, on the car radio of the seed salesman, in the office of the accountant as farmers were counseled to "get big or get out," to expand their production and change their growing practices to participate in a global food system, rather than a regional one. "Feeding the world" was the motto that let Americans turn their heads away from the polluted waters, the increasing severity of floods, soil loss, or the fact that the little farm next door had suddenly disappeared.

But those petro-chemicals and farming practices that feed the world are washing away our topsoil and leaving what remains nutritionally deficient. Ironically, the goal to feed the world has led to a form of agriculture that has made it increasingly difficult for the people of the world to feed themselves. And the fact that fossil fuels are not quite as abundant as they once were, nor as cheap, means that even if we could generate yields of global proportions in perpetuity, we wouldn't be able to deliver the goods in any cost-effective manner.

Can the local, sustainable food movement in the United States feed the world? Hell, no. But ultimately, neither can the industrial agricultural paradigm. No one can feed the world. One country cannot do it, nor can any specific model of production. The earth must be allowed to reclaim its natural productivity. That's why we need local and regional food systems, designed to work harmoniously with local eco-systems. While certain ecological lessons may apply, it would be absurd to think what works for us here in upstate New York for producing food is going to necessarily work in Africa. Heck, many of the methods that work on farms 10 miles from our house won't work on our steep hillside farm. There is no such thing as a universally applicable production practice, nor a universally acceptable diet.

This is not to say that we shouldn't be concerned about global starvation. But if enabling everybody to have access to good, nutritious food is really our goal, we need to look deeper than crop yields and feed-conversion ratios. In addition to the complicated politics involved, we need to examine our individual actions. How are our daily habits impacting humanity's access to a nutritious food supply? Our daily sustenance should not require that other people in the world go without nourishment. Our daily sustenance should not demand excessive fossil fuels for growing, processing and transporting the food to our tables. Beyond that, our consumption habits ideally should not be requiring people in foreign lands to destroy their own access to clean water and fertile soils for the sake of dying our clothing, building our electronics, or making our children's toys.

Feeding the world starts with individual accountability. It needs to be considered in every home, in every business. But the question must be re-framed. Rather than asking farmers if the methods they use can feed the world, we need to look in the mirror and ask ourselves "Do my choices enable the world to feed itself?" If the answer is no, then it is time to make different choices.

There is not one of us who is blameless when the question is re-framed (myself included). But it is not solely up to the farmers to feed the world. It is up to each and every one of us to strive to live a life of personal accountability that will enable this earth to heal, and enable this world to feed itself. And, just as no single agricultural practice will be universally applicable, neither will any single life path. There are many routes to a healed planet. What matters is that we keep asking ourselves to be accountable, and that we keep making the changes that are direly needed. Thus, I leave you with one question: What can you do today that will enable the world to feed itself?

About the Author

*S*hannon Hayes and her husband Bob Hooper live with their two homeschooled children in a solar house deep in the hills of the northern Catskills, where she grew up. They work with her parents on Sap Bush Hollow Farm, raising grassfed and pastured meats, making sausages and pâté, rendering animals fats for soaps, salves and candles, herding honey bees (a fruitless pursuit, but fun to imagine), and marketing their wool crop in the form of blankets and yarn. In 2010 Shannon published *Radical Homemakers*, a controversial bestseller that landed her on the pages of the *New York Times Magazine*, on National Public Radio, and on the pages of countless national and international newspapers and magazines, and even on a few tv spots (she doesn't like to talk about those . . . too embarrassing). In addition, she has written four cookbooks about sustainably-raised meats. *Homespun Mom Comes Unraveled* is her first book of essays, based on her weekly blog, which can be found at ShannonHayes.org (where she sells many of Sap Bush Hollow's non-perishable farm products) and through *Yes!* Magazine at yes.org. Her second book of essays, *From Here*, is due out in 2015. In addition to grilling grassfed burgers, hanging out laundry, and pulling weeds, Hayes is currently at work on her first novel, *Angels and Stones*.

Made in the USA
Lexington, KY
15 November 2014